IMPROVING STUDENT LEARNING AT SCALE

IMPROVING STUDENT LEARNING AT SCALE

A How-To Guide for Higher Education

Keston H. Fulcher and

Caroline O. Prendergast

Foreword by Stephen P. Hundley
Afterword by Natasha A. Jankowski

STERLING, VIRGINIA

COPYRIGHT © 2021 BY STYLUS PUBLISHING, LLC.

Published by Stylus Publishing, LLC.
22883 Quicksilver Drive
Sterling, Virginia 20166-2019

Library of Congress Cataloging-in-Publication Data
Names: Fulcher, Keston H., author. | Prendergast, Caroline, author.
Title: Improving student learning at scale : a how-to guide for higher
    education / Keston H. Fulcher and Caroline O. Prendergast ;
    foreword by Stephen P. Hundley ; afterword by Natasha Jankowski.
Description: First edition | Sterling, Virginia : Stylus Publishing, LLC.,
    2021. | Includes bibliographical references and index. | Summary:
    "This book provides practical strategies for learning improvement,
    enabling faculty to collaborate, and integrating leadership,
    social dynamics, curriculum, pedagogy, assessment, and faculty
    development"-- Provided by publisher.
Identifiers: LCCN 2021017923 (print) | LCCN 2021017924 (ebook) |
    ISBN 9781642671803 (cloth) | ISBN 9781642671810 (paperback) |
    ISBN 9781642671827 (adobe pdf) | ISBN 9781642671834 (epub)
Subjects: LCSH: Education, Higher--United States--Evaluation. |
    Education, Higher--Aims and objectives--United States. | Academic
    achievement--United States. | Holistic education--United States. |
    College teachers--Professional relationships--United States. | College
    teaching--United States. | Educational change--United States.
Classification: LCC LA227.4 .F898 2021 (print) | LCC LA227.4
    (ebook) | DDC 378.73--dc23
LC record available at https://lccn.loc.gov/2021017923
LC ebook record available at https://lccn.loc.gov/2021017924

13-digit ISBN: 978-1-64267-180-3 (cloth)
13-digit ISBN: 978-1-64267-181-0 (paperback)
13-digit ISBN: 978-1-64267-182-7 (library networkable e-edition)
13-digit ISBN: 978-1-64267-183-4 (consumer e-edition)

Printed in the United States of America

All first editions printed on acid-free paper
that meets the American National Standards Institute
Z39-48 Standard.

Bulk Purchases

Quantity discounts are available for use in workshops and for staff development.

Call 1-800-232-0223

First Edition, 2021

We dedicate this book to Megan Good, Kristen Smith, and Chris Coleman: truth seekers willing to imagine a better future for higher education.

CONTENTS

PART THREE: EXPANDING LEARNING IMPROVEMENT AT SCALE

In the United States, we have a dynamic, complex higher education landscape comprised of varying institutional types, each with their own distinct missions, histories, cultures, structures, and resources. Within these institutions, educators offer an array of academic programs, many of which are increasingly organized and delivered in interdisciplinary, experiential, and technology influenced contexts. Individuals and communities attracted to, and served by, our campuses—students, faculty, staff, and external entities—continue to reflect broader societal diversity, including those historically underserved by higher education institutions. This is occurring during a time when colleges and universities have been focusing their attention on addressing pandemic-related needs, responding to national and local cries for racial justice, promoting the value and return-on-investment of a collegiate education to a sometimes-skeptical public, and operating in a sector facing resource constraints, a looming enrollment cliff, and increased global competition.

For those of us working on college and university campuses, these contextual influences require us to be good stewards of the various opportunities we have to facilitate student learning and development. Indeed, we are endeavoring to produce college graduates capable of finding employment, enrolling in advanced higher education programs, pursuing lifelong learning, living and working as civic-minded individuals and professionals in a globally connected world, and remaining involved with us as committed, engaged alumni, among other outcomes. To achieve these outcomes, we develop and implement structured learning opportunities at several touchpoints throughout a student's pathway to graduation, including courses in first-year experiences and general education programs, through focused study within specific academic disciplines, via multidisciplinary collaborations and explorations, and by employing experiential learning opportunities in cocurricular, community, and international contexts.

Designers of these learning opportunities typically set goals for learning, develop evidence-informed interventions to implement them, and routinely assess student achievement of learning—often with the aim of making ongoing improvements to instructional practices and processes based on these outcomes. Using assessment findings to drive meaningful improvements—and doing so in a coordinated, timely manner—has long been a challenge for faculty, staff, and administrators, despite considerable attention given to this issue in the higher education assessment literature. Clearly more work remains to equip our colleagues with the confidence and competence to create improvement-oriented cultures that promote student learning and success. Fortunately, several resources exist to facilitate these efforts, including on-campus professional development opportunities to advance local capabilities, teaching societies within disciplines aimed at enhancing effective disciplinary instruction, and national and international conferences, publications, and associations focused on broader discussions and demonstrations of effective teaching, learning, assessment, and improvement practices.

In addition to being a longtime faculty member and administrator at IUPUI, I have the honor of representing our campus as chair of the Assessment Institute in Indianapolis, the oldest and largest U.S. higher education event focused on assessment and improvement. I also serve as executive editor of *Assessment Update*, a bimonthly periodical from Wiley with a national readership. In October 2019, my IUPUI colleague Susan Kahn and I coedited *Trends in Assessment: Ideas, Opportunities, and Issues for Higher Education* (Stylus), in which more than 40 thought leaders shared perspectives on the future of assessment. More recently, in October 2020 the Assessment Institute launched the *Leading Improvements in Higher Education* podcast, for which I serve as host, where we profile people, initiatives, institutions, and organizations improving conditions in higher education. These collective experiences have afforded me a humbled and unique vantage point to observe several enduring and emerging issues and opportunities related to higher education assessment. One of the emerging opportunities is the need for us to *improve student learning at scale*, in which we move beyond often isolated, fragmented, and incremental changes to create sustained cultures of transformative improvement on our campuses—and, indeed, across the entire higher education sector.

This opportunity—*improving student learning at scale*—is the focus of this specific volume. Keston H. Fulcher and Caroline O. Prendergast make a richly informative and compelling case for why we need to improve student learning at scale, while also providing practical approaches, action steps, and resources to make this a reality in higher education. A key part of their message is the importance of faculty development, collaboration, experimentation, risk taking, and a culture of innovation focused on student learning and reliant on supportive leadership. They begin the book by defining what they mean by *learning, improvement*, and *scale*, including rooting their work in the higher education assessment literature. From there, they proceed with a series of chapters aimed at helping the reader navigate through the learning improvement process—all replete with myriad examples and questions for consideration. While the work of true learning improvement is not easy, especially at the scale advocated by the authors, this volume offers sound, inspiring advice to make the effort more manageable and—dare I say— enjoyable. Readers embarking on this journey can help create a dynamic higher education of the future, one previewed by the authors in chapter 10. Nor should readers do this work in isolation—fortunately, the authors conclude the book with a call to action and an invitation to become part of the larger Learning Improvement Community (https://www.learning-improvement.org/).

Within the higher education ecosystem, each of us has both the privilege and responsibility to promote student learning and success in our individual and collective spheres of influence. We play a role in constructing support- ive environments aimed at producing holistic graduates prepared to thrive and adapt in ever-changing futures. We use evidence-informed interven- tions and innovations throughout the collegiate experience to foster learning and development within and for our students. Finally, we sustain this work through institutional cultures relentlessly focused on continuously improv- ing—at scale—the varying conditions, resources, and experiences for student learning to occur. This book certainly goes a long way toward helping us achieve these purposes.

Stephen P. Hundley
Senior Advisor to the Chancellor and Professor of Organizational
Leadership
IUPUI
Indianapolis, Indiana
March 2021

In 2014, the first author (Fulcher) of this book, along with Megan Good, Chris Coleman, and Kristen Smith (2014) published "A Simple Model for Learning Improvement: Weigh Pig, Feed Pig, Weigh Pig" (affectionately known as the "pig paper"). The premise of the paper was that student learning improvement was rare in higher education, particularly learning improvement *at scale*. Although faculty members at universities across the country expend valuable time and effort to improve teaching in their own course sections, rarely are these efforts unified to span an entire program. In other words, learning improvement "at scale"—efforts that improve the outcomes of all students who complete a degree program or graduate from a university—are exceedingly rare. Two major obstacles stand in the way of widespread improvement: inconsistent definitions and lack of know-how. First, the field of higher education has not yet agreed on criteria for "improvement," resulting in claims of improved student learning that fall apart quickly under scrutiny. Second, little guidance exists for encouraging, fostering, and managing effective improvement efforts. There is no guidebook for improving learning in higher education.

Like Brown and Knight (1994) did before us, the pig paper used an agricultural metaphor—"a pig never fattened because it was weighed"—to explore the role of assessment in improvement efforts. Fulcher et al. (2014) made the parallel argument that students never learned more simply by being assessed.[1] Indeed, the magic ingredient is a better learning environment (more or more nutritional food, in the case of the farm). Key here is the word "better": *Changes* to an educational environment do not necessarily mean students will learn more. To support claims that students learn more from a changed learning environment (i.e., that the new environment represents an *improvement* over the old one), cohorts of students need to be assessed before and after an intervention is implemented. Only when the reassessment shows better learning than the initial assessment can we effectively argue that a change to the educational environment results in improved student learning. This distinction between a change and an improvement is a foundational concept in understanding the need for explicit professional development and support for learning improvement efforts.

Since the publication of the pig paper, we have seen progress. In conversations and presentations at conferences, we have noticed fewer people confusing changes with improvement. Further, efforts at our home institution and beyond have shown a growing community of higher educators who are attempting to learn how to improve student learning and increase interest in the movement. At James Madison University (JMU), we have piloted three learning improvement projects in academic degree programs, and we are developing a campus-wide learning improvement project as we write this book. Additionally, we have uncovered a few examples of legitimate improvement at scale over the last 2 decades. Furthermore, JMU faculty and graduate students have published two dissertations and written several articles on the topic of learning improvement in academic and student affairs (e.g., Good, 2015; Lending et al., 2018; Smith, 2017; Smith et al., 2019).

In an effort to ignite a larger discussion, JMU and the Center of Inquiry at Wabash College launched the first Learning Improvement Summit in 2017 (Horst & Ames, 2018), which brought together two dozen thought leaders in higher education. While the group agreed that learning improvement was important, there was much debate about how higher education should proceed. Nevertheless, themes emerged regarding what might be needed to move forward: an operational definition of *improvement;* an integration of faculty development, assessment, and day-to-day faculty activities; discussion about if and how accreditation should link to improvement efforts; examples of learning improvement to be used as models; and educational resources for stakeholders interested in learning improvement efforts.

Two summits have convened since, largely focused on the themes identified in the first summit. From these meetings and other conversations at a number of assessment conferences, Monica Stitt-Bergh of the University of Hawai'i at Mānoa launched the Learning Improvement Community (n.d.), composed primarily of professionals working as assessment directors or faculty developers within colleges. The purpose of this group is to

> promote student learning improvement in higher education, with a focus on program and institution levels. We explore how thoughtful changes to learning environments can improve learning and how learning assessment can support and document such efforts. We encourage the disaggregation of findings on student learning to answer questions regarding equity in learning for all groups of students. (Paras 1–2)

The group has collected learning improvement stories from several institutions and published them on their website. The Learning Improvement

Community is quickly becoming a hub of the higher education learning improvement movement in the United States.

Several other schools, including Auburn University, Arkansas State, Longwood University, and Purdue University Fort Wayne, have established support for learning improvement. For example, Auburn's assessment and faculty development offices are working together to support six different programs in learning improvement. Additionally, Auburn has a webpage devoted to learning improvement resources for all faculty.

While progress toward enacting and documenting learning improvement has been made, we hope to accelerate the speed by which institutions of higher education embrace and successfully implement improvement efforts. The purpose of this book is to provide the necessary guidance for launching improvement efforts. The learning improvement knowledge base is constantly expanding, but up to this point, much of the work has focused on critical components of learning improvement (e.g., assessment, faculty development, cognition) in isolation. Other efforts have focused on large-scale improvement efforts, but not in the context of higher education. We endeavor to curate the existing knowledge about, and strategy for, improvement in this how-to book for successfully implementing learning improvement at a broader scale in higher education.

What Will (and Won't) This Book Do?

This book helps readers integrate the components of modern college structures into an effective learning system that can foster the improvement of student learning. As such, the focus of the book is to paint a picture of what successful learning improvement looks like, the processes and people that support the system, and the resources needed to make it happen. As important, we also detail how the system can falter. We often learn a great deal about how something ought to work by understanding how it breaks down. We hope you will use the contents of this book as a road map for tackling problems and proposing bold new solutions that result in improved student learning at scale.

This book aims to show how assessment, faculty development, educational research, change theory, and leadership can, when woven together, create strong foundations for effective student learning and improvement efforts. While knowledge of these areas is necessary for shepherding learning improvement projects, we will not delve deeply into these topics.

We have intentionally focused this book on improving student learning and development. These are the things that students should know, think, or do as a function of their educational experiences. This lens is one of parsimony and not of necessity: We expect that many of the concepts could be adapted to related institutional effectiveness areas (e.g., satisfaction, retention, and graduation rates). Moreover, we intentionally chose to focus on student learning within the academic division. Nevertheless, we provide an example in Appendix A to illustrate how the principles can be applied to student affairs as well.

Who Is This Book For?

Faculty members are the drivers of learning improvement efforts. Their proximity to students and their position as educators equip them, more so than any other group, to understand what students need and where students are falling short. This book will provide faculty teams with tools to evaluate their programs, plan for (and implement) change, and effectively assess student learning and development.

This book is intended specifically for the talented, ambitious faculty who have at least moderate knowledge of pedagogy, assessment, curriculum, and structures of academic degree programs. These faculty members have read books or attended workshops related to best practices in teaching. They have had success making intentional, targeted changes to their own courses and seen positive results. They have contributed to program-level assessment. They have created tests. They are cognizant that what happens in courses before or after their own matters to student learning. In many instances, they are active consumers of (or contributors to) the scholarship of teaching and learning. This book helps these individuals have a greater impact on more students through collaboration with teams of like-minded colleagues. Frankly, if the book doesn't reach this audience, we've failed.

The next intended audience members are assessment professionals, faculty developers, and administrators in the academic division. They are responsible for providing the institutional support for program- and institution-level improvement efforts. This book gives them a sense of how to work together to create an environment that fosters ambitious, successful learning improvement projects. While it is true that successful learning improvement efforts start with the will of the faculty, it is also true that most such efforts will be limited without strategic support from the administration.

Assessment professionals, too, can benefit from the ideas in this book because of the interconnected histories of improvement efforts in higher education and the growth of formalized assessment systems. Writ large, the two purposes of assessment are accountability and improved learning (Ewell,

2009). We do not anticipate surprising any of our readers by reminding them that higher education has demonstrated meager evidence of improving student learning, and assessment is often blamed for this shortcoming. Therefore, this book illustrates how assessment can—and should—be integrated with improvement efforts.

The ideas discussed in this book will help faculty developers connect their work more directly with program- and institution-level student learning improvement. While these professionals help faculty make learning environments better, the scale at which they work is typically localized in individual course sections. Furthermore, faculty developers are often called upon to show the impact of their work.

Faculty developers and assessment professionals alike are realizing that integrating their services can ultimately benefit student learning (e.g., Kinzie et al., 2019; Reder & Crimmins, 2018). Faculty developers provide the space and environment where faculty can grow as instructors, and assessment professionals possess the tools to measure impact on student learning. Together, their expertise provides crucial support for effective teaching and learning. The ideas in this book will guide faculty developers and assessment professionals in the development of effective partnerships to enact (and document the impact of) large-scale learning improvement efforts.

Finally, institutions' senior leaders are often the people on the hook for demonstrating and improving educational quality. Imagine that the senior leadership of a university is given the tools to help support successful learning improvement efforts that affect dozens, hundreds, or thousands of students. If they understand the overall improvement process, the resources it requires, and the centrality of strong administrative support, they can create the overall environment to make learning improvement projects commonplace and successful.

This book provides a new vision for the structure of university improvement efforts. We believe that the learning improvement framework offers a novel, effective approach to the age-old question: How can we do better? Administrators play a crucial role in the mechanics of higher education, and we anticipate that this book will offer a useful approach to strategic, targeted, intentional improvement.

We hope that this book helps you become more effective in your own role. Perhaps some of you will join us in expanding the learning improvement movement within your institutions and organizations. From the outset, we wish to acknowledge that achieving learning improvement at scale is difficult. In fact, in the beginning, we experienced more setbacks than successes. Nevertheless, we learned from the missteps and victories alike, and we have become more effective within our own improvement efforts. Over time, our successes have become bigger and more predictable, and our setbacks less catastrophic. The tools that have taken us the better part of a decade to curate and develop will not guarantee instant success for you, but they will hasten your (and your institution's) ability to improve. In our opinion, the potential positive outcomes for students more than make up for the considerable effort. We thank you for embarking on this journey with us.

Note

1   As a point of clarification, individual students can benefit from the process of regular testing and feedback about their performance (e.g., Halpern & Hakel, 2003). However, educational systems *themselves* do not become better at educating students just because assessment systems are implemented to measure their effectiveness. This shift from a focus on individual students to a focus on learning systems will be repeated throughout this volume.

ACKNOWLEDGMENTS

This book is inspired and influenced by many of our colleagues, friends, and loved ones. Some helped us pose better questions, others helped us integrate concepts, and dozens helped us learn through trial and error. Without them, this book would not exist.

Our colleague Sara Finney was the first to help us connect the concepts of program theory, interventions, and implementation fidelity with assessment. Her knack for understanding the components of complex systems and her relentless pursuit of excellence drive us—and everyone who counts her as a colleague and friend—to keep chipping away at our field's most persistent problems.

Diane Lending and Tom Dillon served as our inspiration for Xela and Rusty, this book's fictional improvement protagonists, who first appear in chapter 2. They and their collaborative colleagues in JMU's Computer Information Systems program gave us a glimpse of how thoughtful strategy, hard work, and collegiality could transform students for the better.

Bill Hawk, Christian Early, and Lori Pyle from JMU's Ethical Reasoning in Action office have generously offered their support to various projects, including several dissertations that have helped us study ethical reasoning and learning improvement simultaneously. Andrea Pope was, among innumerable other contributions, the chief facilitator of a 3-day learning improvement workshop on ethical reasoning from Indiana University–Purdue University Indianapolis, the University of Hawaiʻi, and the University of North Carolina at Charlotte. We thank Shaun Boyne, Christine Robinson, and Monica Stitt-Bergh for wrangling—and fearlessly leading—learning improvement teams from their institutions. Liz Sanchez also contributed substantially to learning improvement and ethical reasoning through several projects and publications (and through her thoughtful feedback on an early draft of this book).

Our partners in JMU's Center for Faculty Innovation (CFI) have provided endless guidance in navigating and developing learning improvement support for faculty. Cara Meixner, the CFI's executive director, deserves special recognition for helping us think through learning improvement from a faculty development lens as well as partnering with us on several projects. Former executive director Carol Hurney was integral in setting up the early infrastructure for learning improvement. And, Steve Harper has been a thoughtful partner for many years.

Many other administrators and graduate students at JMU have also been supportive of our learning improvement investigations. Jerry Benson, Heather Coltman, Linda Halpern, and Marilou Johnson created a supportive environment for assessment and faculty development to work together. The faculty from the Communication Studies, Physics, and Writing, Rhetoric, and Technical Communication programs have all advanced our thinking about learning improvement. Donna Sundre, former executive director of assessment at CARS helped make some initial contacts. Thomas Hartka, Liz Spratto, and David Yang helped us be creative by developing a learning improvement game. Madison Holzman, Yelisey Shapovalov, and Rebecca Simmons provided excellent insight regarding how improvement might be taught better. Kurt Schick has provided support in countless forms, from his leadership in an ambitious learning improvement project to a decade of invaluable mentorship to the second author.

Ray Van Dyke from Weave was one of the first to embrace the concept of learning improvement. We appreciate the support and opportunities he has provided over the years.

Several colleagues in the United States, and across the world, have also helped create learning improvement conversations that cross institutional boundaries. Allison Ames, Charlie Blaich, Jeanne Horst, Paula Love, and Kathy Wise were instrumental in convening the first Learning Improvement Summit, which saw experts from assessment, faculty development, and accreditation gather to think about how learning improvement intersects with the rest of higher education.

From the learning improvement summits, Monica Stitt-Bergh has led the charge in creating a new organization, the Learning Improvement Community, which has set the wheels in motion for expanding learning improvement in the United States. We appreciate her leadership, tenacity, and friendship. Others who have contributed include Mays Amad, Gianina Baker, Katie Boyd, Cynthia Crimmins, Jodi Fisler, Kathleen Gorski, Laura Harrington, Yao Hill, Kelsey Kirland, Jason Lyons, Lee Rakes, Michael Reder, Linda Townsend, Pam Tracy, and Andrea Willis.

Assessment-related organizations have also been wonderful partners over the years. Gianina Baker, Natasha Jankowski, Jillian Kinzie, and Erick Montenegro from the National Institute for Learning Outcomes Assessment (NILOA) have deepened our thinking through numerous partnerships. Kate McConnell from Association of American Colleges & Universities (AAC&U) has made us think through how learning improvement might intersect with the VALUE rubrics. Robin Anderson, Josh Brown, and Nick

Curtis have supported learning improvement through Virginia Assessment Group's *Research and Practice in Assessment* journal. Several of these leaders have also participated in the Learning Improvement Summits and the Learning Improvement Community as well.

The regional accreditors have been allies. The Southern Association of Colleges and Schools Commission on Colleges' (SACSCOC's) Quality Enhancement Plan sparked our thinking about how to improve learning at scale. Furthermore, Alexei Matveev and Belle Wheelan have provided excellent opportunities for several graduate students interested in seeing how the worlds of accountability and improvement intertwine. New England Commission of Higher Education's (NECHE's) Barbara Brittingham attended the first Learning Improvement Summit. Last, David Chase from Western Association of Schools and Colleges (WASC) has been forward thinking in incorporating learning improvement into WASC professional development.

Many non-U.S. scholars and practitioners have helped us learn about assessment and improvement in their respective countries: Fabio Arico, Sally Brown, Satako Fukahori, Amani Hamdan, Peter Hartley, Tansy Jessop, Phil Knight, Kayo Matsushita, Erica Morris, Margaret Price, Susan Orr, Kay Sambell, Mark Schofield, and Naomi Winstone.

The concept of learning improvement in higher education is not new. Since the 1980s, many of assessment's early pioneers have spoken vigorously about the importance of integrating assessment with improvement. We thank Thomas Angelo, Trudy Banta, Peter Ewell, George Kuh, Peggy Maki, and Linda Suskie for their foundational work. We owe a nod of appreciation to T. Dary Erwin who, more than 30 years ago, created a space at JMU to investigate and improve learning.

Special thanks go to Stephen Hundley, Pat Hutchings, and Marsha Lovett who reviewed an early draft of the book and who have been supportive in many other ways over the years, and to David Brightman from Stylus, who patiently walked us through each step of the authoring and publication process.

Finally, we would like to thank the many people in our lives—outside of the walls of our office—who have provided essential support, grounding, and levity over the course of this book's development. Gabe Huck and Theresa Kubasak provided consistent reminders of the power of writing and the criticality of education, their incisive calls for action always punctuated with laughter and sustenance. Becca Howes-Mischel, Katherine Reynolds, and Andrea Russell provided unwavering encouragement through the joys and frustrations of writing. Paige, Susie, and Steve Evans, along with David, JoAnne, and Gregory Prendergast, have nurtured a deep appreciation for the pursuit of knowledge, and will likely be pleased that we can now hold conversations that do not include, "So, how's that book going?" Brian Dempsey, Javarro Russell, and John Willse provided virtual happy hour respites by discussing important pop culture topics like the Equalizer, Airwolf, and the Notorious B.I.G. Finally, we thank our spouses, Meghan Schenker-Fulcher and Taylor Evans, for their patience and support through this long journey of book writing.

PART ONE

INTRODUCTION TO LEARNING IMPROVEMENT AT SCALE

LAYING OUT THE PROBLEM

Despite the decades-long history of assessment in higher education, little evidence indicates that assessment results in improved student learning. To understand why this is the case, we must first develop a common language for discussing learning improvement at scale. We then provide a historical overview of higher education and the assessment thereof and provide explanations for the lack of evidence of learning improvement in higher education. The chapter concludes with an outline of this book's structure, mission, and goals.

What Is Learning Improvement at Scale?

This book is a step-by-step guide for improving student learning in higher education. We focus on improvement efforts at scale. Each of these terms—*student learning*, *improvement*, and *at scale*—requires explanation.

By *learning*, we mean the knowledge, skills, and attitudes that students acquire through education. Learning can occur in broad, general areas like writing, ethical reasoning, art appreciation, and oral communication. Learning can also occur in discipline-specific areas like functional anatomy, corporate law, fluid dynamics, and sculpting, or in attitudinal and behavioral domains such as sense of belongingness and ability to collaborate with diverse peer groups.

By *improvement*, we mean demonstrated increases in student knowledge, skills, and attitudes due to changes in the learning environment (throughout this book, we will refer to these changes as *interventions*). Of note, to move the needle on skills like ethical reasoning or corporate law requires powerful intervention that often spans multiple courses.

To demonstrate such improvement, one must gather baseline data, change the learning environment, and reassess to determine student proficiency under the new learning environment. The comparison of the baseline data and the reassessment must show that students who experienced the changed learning environment perform better than students who did not. We refer to this general methodology—assess, intervene, reassess—as the *simple model for learning improvement* (Fulcher et al., 2014).

As a basic example, imagine that biology faculty were concerned with the bone-identifying abilities of students graduating from their program. They presented senior students with a computer-based skeleton model and asked them to identify as many bones as they could. On average, suppose that they found the assessed group of seniors were able to identify 135 out of 206 bones. This measurement would provide the baseline estimate of student bone-identification proficiency. The faculty could then modify the curriculum, emphasizing practice with identifying bones and providing feedback about students' bone-identifying abilities (constituting a change in learning environment). Then, imagine that the next cohort of students, all of whom had experienced the new curriculum, was reassessed and found to be able to identify an average of 197 bones. This would represent a 62-bone improvement over the previous cohort (i.e., the reassessment showed better performance). In this situation, the evidence would demonstrate that learning improvement has occurred.

In earlier work, we noted that higher educators often confuse the words *change* and *improvement* (Fulcher et al., 2014). People are often excited to label as an "improvement" any modification assumed or expected to be useful, even in the absence of proof that the modification leads to a better outcome than its predecessor. Using the bone identification example, the faculty members might prematurely (and incorrectly) claim that learning improvement has taken place as soon as curricular modifications are made. However, we would argue that faculty members merely made a *change* to the learning environment at that point. Only after reassessment demonstrates better learning (the 62-bone increase in students' average identification ability) than occurred under the old curriculum can faculty claim that the change had actually been an *improvement*.

We have also found that the issue of scale is often overlooked in improvement efforts. While individual faculty members frequently work to make their courses better, coordinated efforts that stretch across entire academic programs are much more rare. When we refer to learning improvement "at scale", we mean improvement efforts that span an entire program, affecting all affiliated students. What is considered a "program" is likely to vary across institutions.

For the purposes of this book, we consider "programs" to be academic structures that have the following characteristics:

- They require a consistent set of experiences, such as a set of mandatory core courses.
- They require students to engage with the set of experiences over an extended time period (usually multiple semesters).
- They are intentionally structured to achieve some outcome (or, more likely some set of multiple outcomes).

Generally, when we discuss academic programs, we intend for our readers to envision academic degree programs or general education programs. University structures, of course, are widely varied; other types of programs, such as some academic minors, may very well fit these requirements. Similarly, some academic degree programs might not fit these requirements (e.g., customizable majors with few or no required courses or predetermined outcomes).

Given a simple program structure, it is technically possible to achieve learning improvement at scale with a single section of one course. For instance, imagine a small program that graduates 20 students per year. Many of the courses consist of only one section taught by one faculty member. If an instructor in such a position made a change to the learning environment in the single course section, all 20 students would be affected. In this special case, making a change to one course section affects all students in the program. If those students did learn more as a function of this change, then learning improvement at scale would be achieved.

While we acknowledge this possibility, we emphasize more complicated learning improvement at-scale efforts. We find that faculty and administrators particularly struggle to conceptualize and implement multisection, multicourse improvement efforts. Further, for many complex skills like writing, students benefit from exposure to vertical interventions weaving through multiple courses throughout a program's curriculum. It is unsurprising that ambitious, wide-reaching improvement efforts like these would pose difficulty in their organization and implementation. This is precisely the problem we hope to address. Thus, this book especially emphasizes the strategies associated with complex cases of learning improvement at scale.

Let's continue with the biology example to illustrate an effort that occurs at scale with a complex structure. The biology program graduates 150 students per year; therefore, learning improvement at scale should focus on developing and implementing interventions that affect all 150 students. Furthermore, the faculty felt that the skill was challenging enough that it could not be adequately addressed in just one course. Therefore, the proposed interventions for bone identification spanned two required courses, 101 and 102. Further, imagine that each of those courses is composed of three sections (each of which enrolls 50 students), and that these six sections are taught by six different faculty members. This scenario is displayed visually in Figure 1.1. Each oval represents a different faculty member, while each rectangle represents a different course section.

In this context, pursuing learning improvement at scale would require all six faculty to integrate their work through a process we will refer to throughout this book as *alignment*. Faculty demonstrating alignment are coordinated with each other in their approach to teaching. *Horizontal alignment* means that all faculty teaching sections within the same course work collaboratively and have agreed on a common set of outcomes and common strategies to accomplish these outcomes. In our biology example, the three faculty members teaching 101 would need to demonstrate horizontal alignment with each other, as would the three faculty members teaching 102. In Figure 1.1, horizontal alignment is demonstrated by the dotted horizontal lines linking across sections within a course. Note that horizontal alignment can be viewed on a spectrum where utter alignment means every faculty member does everything in a lock-step manner (which we rarely advocate). On the other extreme, with no alignment, sections bear almost no resemblance except for the course name.

Vertical alignment refers to the connection among sequential courses that are meant to build on one another in the service of program-level outcomes. In Figure 1.1, vertical alignment is demonstrated by the dotted vertical lines lining sections of 101 with sections of 102 (note that this is, of course, a simplified visual representation: *All* sections of 101 would need to be vertically aligned with *all* sections of 102, necessitating strong horizontal alignment

Figure 1.1. Horizontal and vertical alignment.

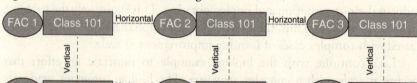

Source: Fulcher, K. H., & Prendergast, C. O. (2019). Lots of assessment, little improvement? How to fix the broken system. In S. P. Hundley & S. Kahn (Eds.), *Trends in assessment: Ideas, opportunities, and issues for higher education* (p. 169). Stylus.

between sections within each course). Strong vertical alignment enables seamless scaffolding as a student progresses through a program. Faculty members in earlier courses prepare students for downstream success. And, faculty in later courses of a sequence can count on students having certain skills when they enter the classroom.

In this case, no single faculty member would have the ability to improve the learning of all students. For example, if only faculty member 2 (who teaches 101, section B) made substantial adjustments to her section, only 50 of 150 students would be affected. Although faculty member 2 would deserve commendation, learning improvement *at scale* would not be achieved. Only one third of the students would receive an intervention. Furthermore, even those students would have only received the intervention in one course (101), not in both courses (101 and 102) as intended.

Now, imagine if a learning improvement initiative were attempted for all undergraduates of an institution. If 1,000 students are in each graduating cohort, then the interventions would need to reach all 1,000 students. As opposed to six faculty members, as in the biology example, dozens of faculty members would likely need to coordinate with each other. This kind of large-scale collaboration is necessary for most learning improvement initiatives, and it is with these situations in mind that this book was written. The subsequent chapters will attempt to illuminate considerations and strategies for implementing program-wide improvement efforts.

Contrasting Our Purpose With Another Type of Improvement

In the assessment literature, a growing trend is to speak of "real-time" assessment (Maki, 2017). The thrust of real-time assessment is to focus on current students by collecting data and making changes to the learning environments the students experience. This differs from the type of improvement discussed in this book, which involves collecting data on current students as a baseline, and then making changes to the learning environments that affect *future* students.

We acknowledge that institutions and the faculty and staff within them should do what they can to help current students. Research has demonstrated the benefits of consistent, timely, and explicit feedback for students' learning (e.g., Evans, 2013; Halpern & Hakel, 2003). Nevertheless, in some circumstances, "real-time" change efforts are not feasible. As a rule of thumb, the larger and more comprehensive a learning improvement effort, the less likely a real-time approach is to work. The following four learning scenarios, loosely based on our own experiences, illustrate this point.

Scenario 1

Two instructors collaborate to teach the two sections of an introductory statistics course. Weekly, they administer cognitive checks to gauge students' learning. The instructors find that most of their students struggle to differentiate the standard deviation from the standard error of the mean. The faculty assign a short video that differentiates the concepts, and then have all the students email the instructors a brief description of the difference between the two concepts in their own words. A few weeks later, 90% of students correctly explain the concept on the midterm exam. This is an example where an initial assessment and pointed feedback likely contributed to better learning by the same set of students. In other words, real-time assessment is working as it should.

Scenario 2

The same two faculty as in scenario 1 receive disconcerting news midway through the course. A colleague who runs the department roundtable noticed a hole in students' statistics skills. The colleague, playing the part of a client, asks the students to explain various parts of statistical output (a common situation for real-life statistical consultants). The concepts were basic, and all students should have learned them, but in this context they struggled mightily. Other faculty who were at the meeting confirmed the sobering news.

Upon reflection, this result was not a surprise. The way students were being taught in this class was not aligned with the important, real-world task the students were asked to complete during the roundtable discussion. This problem clearly could not be fixed in a few minutes or even a few hours of instruction. The instructors participated in an extended course redesign process during the following summer. There, they incorporated considerable structural changes to the course to address the weakness. The revision helped the next cohort of students to respond more readily and accurately to the statistical role-playing task.

Scenario 3

All faculty members in a graduate psychology program meet at the end of each semester to evaluate every student. Where are they strong? Where are they weak? Are they on track to finish their degree? If not, what problems need to be addressed? What is the program's strategy of giving each student feedback about their performance? What does each adviser need to work on to support their students? The goal is to catch students before they veer too far off track.

Scenario 4

Prodded by its regional accreditor, university officials endeavored to improve the ethical reasoning skills of their university's 20,000 undergraduate students. At the initial stages, the university did not have a common definition of *ethical reasoning,* did not know which colleges and departments desired to be part of the project, did not have assessment instruments, did not have a grasp of current ethical reasoning programs and pedagogy across campus, did not know what interventions were effective in improving students ethical reasoning skills, and had few faculty and staff trained in teaching ethical reasoning. A group of faculty and staff members across the university set to work developing interventions, providing professional development to instructors, and creating assessment tools.

Unsurprisingly, only in the 4th year of this project did changes to the learning environment begin affecting students' ethical reasoning skills. In other words, students did not demonstrate improved ethical reasoning skills until three cohorts after the identification of the improvement project. At the outset, the institution was years away from providing real-time assessment and improvement to the initial cohort of students. The underlying learning architecture needed to be built first.

Focus on Learning Improvement

This book is aimed to help higher education practitioners think about the large-scale, complex learning improvement projects akin to the situations described in scenarios 2 and 4, although we commend and endorse the type of real-time assessment illustrated in scenarios 1 and 3. Improving student learning and development throughout campuses and across the country will require a variety of approaches and a broad base of expertise. In this text, we will focus on the area we see as underdeveloped—learning improvement at scale over the course of multiple student cohorts—not because it is the only tool necessary for colleges and universities, but because it is the area we see as in most urgent need of attention and development.

The Interconnected Worlds of Accountability and Improvement

The history of American higher education demonstrates that there has likely never been a time during which the worth and methods of a college education evaded public scrutiny. Controversy over what should be taught in universities—and how that teaching should take place—has been one of the system's few constants. Up until the end of World War II, higher education primarily served the children of the nation's elite (Bok, 2008). Memorization of classic texts and translations of ancient languages were the norm, as was tension between students and faculty over the merits of this sort of study (Thelin & Hirschy, 2009). These arguments took place in the most revered American colleges and universities, including Columbia and Yale (Bok, 2008; Thelin & Hirschy, 2009). By the late 19th century, Dartmouth students and alumni were so infuriated by college president Samuel Bartlett's refusal to modernize the curriculum (through the addition of courses in the natural and physical sciences, history, and economics, among others) that they put him on trial, leading to his eventual removal from his position (Thelin & Hirschy, 2009).

Academics began to question higher education's purpose: Was it to develop morally "good" people or was it to prepare students to become workers? How faculty and administrators viewed this question greatly influenced how courses were established and navigated by students. At the turn of the 20th century, curricula varied widely across colleges. Some favored traditionally "academic" courses (e.g., classical languages) while others favored more practical courses intended to impart vocational skills (Bok, 2008; Thelin & Hirschy, 2009). Some schools had strict course sequencing while others consisted of almost all electives (Bok, 2008; Thelin & Hirschy, 2009). These debates live on today.

What was being taught, however, was not the only consideration. Scholars like John Dewey (1923) drew attention to *how* students were taught. He was an early advocate of "learning by doing" as opposed to strictly memorizing information from texts. Despite the 19th- and early-20th-century musings, it wasn't until the 1980s that policymakers began conceptualizing student learning as a quality indicator by which to evaluate colleges (Study Group on the Conditions of Excellence in American Higher Education, 1984). Alexander Astin (1985) pioneered the belief that higher education should be evaluated on *talent development*, which he defined as "changes in the student from the beginning to the end of an educational program. These changes can cover a wide range of cognitive and affective attributes" (p. 61). In other words, Astin was interested in *student learning outcomes* (SLOs). Up to that point, institutional quality was evaluated almost entirely on inputs (e.g., number of faculty holding doctoral degrees, test scores of incoming students) and outputs (e.g., graduation rates, employment rates of graduates). By the early 1990s, the amount and quality of student learning had been institutionalized as an indicator of quality. The federal government—through regional accreditors—mandated that higher education institutions report learning outcomes assessment results to demonstrate educational quality (Ewell, 2009). By requiring institutions to earn and maintain accreditation in order to receive federal education funding in the form of federal student loans, regional accreditation policy serves as a powerful force for transmitting government policy into university mandates.

Undergirding these quality assurance efforts is the premise of continuous improvement. Colleges are expected to make the learning environment better by responding to assessment results. How (and how clearly) *improvement* is defined varies across accrediting bodies (Smith et al., 2015), but the common spirit is that student learning should be progressively getting better through colleges' efforts. It is worth noting that this goes beyond the expectation that students will know more at graduation than they did upon college entry. Rather, the notion of continuous improvement calls for each successive cohort of students to graduate having learned more than the cohort before. In other words, the institution is expected to continuously improve its programming, as demonstrated by the consistently increasing skills of graduates. To provide a sense of scope of the reach of accreditation policies, the regional accreditors are responsible for approximately 3,000 U.S. colleges (Council of Regional Accrediting Commissions, n.d.). By extension, accreditors and their policies influence hundreds of thousands of academic degree and certificate programs, and over 1.5 million faculty therein (National Center for Education Statistics, 2020).

At the same time accreditation requirements began to mandate new kinds of assessment efforts, institutions began making structural changes to support student learning. Colleges had begun to establish faculty development offices in the 1960s and 1970s, but most faculty development was assumed to take place during periods of unpaid leave (McKee et al., 2013). The faculty development offices that did exist were largely technology centered, serving as resources for audiovisual support in the classroom (North & Scholl, 1979). By the early 2000s, such offices had proliferated in colleges around the United States (Lewis, 2010). Assessment offices, too, began to appear in universities around the 1980s.

According to Ewell (2002), the first assessment practitioners in higher education faced multiple hurdles. They lacked shared language, quality assessment measures, and expertise. In fact, he referred to these early assessment adopters as "happy amateurs" (Hutchings & Marchese, 1990). In the intervening decades, both faculty development and assessment have become more sophisticated (Beach et al., 2016; Ewell, 2009; Jankowski et al., 2018). Professional organizations, scholarly outlets, and professional development opportunities have emerged to support these maturing fields. The tools at their disposal, including instructional technology and assessment instruments, have advanced and diversified.

Radical shifts have also occurred in the structures and entities linking universities in the intervening decades. With institutional, regional, and national support networks emphasizing the importance of high-quality teaching and assessment (and accreditation standards requiring the same), universities have more support for learning and higher expectations for assessment quality. On the surface, there is reason to assume that assessment results are being used for learning improvement, as the accreditors intend. If regional accreditors are "requiring" evidence of assessment as well as improvements based on assessment, we would expect every institution to have its fair share of program-level improvement examples by now. Indeed, a recent national study found that chief academic officers reported using assessment for program improvement "quite a bit" (Jankowski et al., 2018).

Unfortunately, a more careful investigation reveals that surface impressions do not reflect reality. Conducting assessment with the intent of improving, while noble, is not the same thing as actually improving student learning. Jankowski et al. (2018) did not mince words:

> While use of assessment results is increasing, documenting improvements in student learning and the quality of teaching falls short of what the enterprise needs. Provosts provided numerous examples of expansive changes at their institutions drawing on assessment data, but too few had examples of whether the changes had the intended effects. (p. 26)

In other words, the assumed "improvements" are not accompanied by evidence of increased student learning or development.

To further illustrate the point, Trudy Banta and Charlie Blaich (2011) were asked to write an article in *Change* magazine highlighting institutional examples of assessment leading to learning improvement. These experts—two of the best-known in higher education—could not find enough examples to write the article as intended. Instead, the article morphed into an essay describing obstacles to learning improvement.

Leaders in faculty development have noted a parallel challenge. At about the same time that Ewell was reflecting on the lack of learning improvement from the assessment perspective, Angelo (2000) provided a similar critique of faculty development:

> Since the beginnings of the current higher education reform movement in the mid-1980s thousands of American faculty developers, administrators, and faculty leaders have promoted change under the banners of assessment, continuous quality improvement, active learning, strategic planning, distance education, and other related movements. Much has changed as a result of their efforts and much has improved, of course. Nonetheless, there are still surprisingly few well-documented examples of significant, lasting gains in student learning at the department or

institutional level. More broadly, nearly 30 years of organized faculty development efforts in the US have reaped rather modest rewards, if evidence of improved student learning is the relevant indicator. (p. 98)

According to Condon et al. (2016), this problem still persists. To contextualize the lack-of-learning-improvement issue, Condon et al. (2016) offered a logic model of how faculty development should impact student learning:

Step 1: Faculty member participates in professional development.
Step 2: Faculty member learns how to teach better.
Step 3: Faculty member integrates better teaching approach in course section(s).
Step 4: Students learn better as a function of the improved learning environment.

Condon et al. (2016) point out that the evidence supporting the logic model becomes scarcer and scarcer progressing from step 1 to step 4: Plentiful evidence exists for participation rates in faculty development (step 1), but evidence is scant that student learning improves as a result of faculty development (step 4). Steinert et al.'s (2016) review of faculty development studies in medical programs further reinforces that evidence of learning improvement is rarely investigated in faculty development. Only five of the 111 studies the authors reviewed examined changes to student learning (i.e., Condon et al.'s (2016) fourth step).

Concerns about learning improvement have been voiced beyond circles of assessment experts and faculty developers. For example, *The Chronicle of Higher Education* and the *New York Times* recently published editorials critiquing assessment on several fronts, including its inability to make higher education better (Gilbert, 2015, 2018; Worthen, 2018). The *Washington Post* featured two articles about the wastefulness of teacher training in K–12 settings (Layton, 2015; Strauss, 2014).

For clarity's sake, a lack of learning improvement at scale is *not* merely an assessment concern, a faculty development concern, or even a higher education concern. We argue that it is a societal concern. Educational experiences and, by proxy, learning have been linked to downstream benefits for individuals like higher-paying jobs, greater lifetime earnings, and even greater well-being (Daly & Bengali, 2014; Ray & Kafka, 2014). At aggregated levels, similar patterns hold. A country's economic wealth is correlated positively with the education level of its citizens (Hanushek & Woessmann, 2010). In the United States, the average college graduate contributes over a quarter of a million dollars more in lifetime taxes than the average high school graduate without a college education while receiving far less money in direct financial benefits from the government (Trostel, 2015). In other words, college-educated people present a net benefit to the health of the U.S. tax base. College graduates are also more likely than nongraduates to volunteer, work in the nonprofit sector, and donate to charity (Trostel, 2015). It stands to reason that better learning outcomes can be expected to positively affect individuals and society.

However, the benefits of higher education should not be taken for granted. Like Jankowski and Marshall (2017), we believe it is our responsibility to continuously seek improvements to higher education by striving to create systems in which students can learn more effectively. Without ongoing learning improvement, these benefits will eventually become stale as we fail to adapt to changing economies and sociopolitical landscapes. Improvement, then, should be every college's explicit mandate rather than the rarity it is today. This book proposes solutions by which higher educators can address the lack of improvement in our current learning systems. Given that every institution is supposed to show learning improvement but virtually none does, this is a problem faced by millions of faculty, staff, and administrators. But before offering solutions, we need to provide a deeper description of the problem.

Why Is Learning Improvement So Evasive?

Recall the story of Banta and Blaich (2011), who scoured the national landscape for examples of assessment leading to learning improvement in higher education. After coming up short, they decided instead to examine *why* learning improvement might be so rare. They began by first acknowledging that engaging faculty is critical: Faculty create the space where learning happens, so their involvement in the assessment and improvement processes is non-negotiable. They then listed three specific obstacles to learning improvement. First, they argued that external mandates don't facilitate campus engagement. If faculty feel that the pressure to improve is coming from outsiders, they may respond in a minimalist fashion: What's the least we have to do to keep the accreditors at bay? As Banta and Blaich (2011) argue, "Whether institutions are building their own assessment measures or adopting standardized measures, the key is to build the connection to local campus concerns intentionally" (p. 25).

Second, they pointed out that turnover rates are high in faculty and administrative leadership for assessment. Good assessment and learning improvement require consistent leadership. In reality, leadership is often in flux, from presidents to provosts, to institution-level assessment directors, to the assessment coordinators within programs. How can faculty be expected to use assessment results when the expectations for assessment frequently change? For example, the first author consulted with an institution that had three different university assessment directors in 5 years. Each had a different approach and different expectations for assessment. The faculty wondered how they could work on improving their program when they were constantly trying to figure out the assessment expectations. Their experiences were not isolated. Banta and Blaich (2011) argue that "changes in administrative leadership, faculty, and staff often have a more profound impact on institutional assessment work than on other functions. . . . This shows that using evidence to promote improvement is not yet a core institutional function" (p. 26).

Third, they argued that timelines for change are often unrealistic. Banta and Blaich (2011) recognize that the mere act of carefully collecting and reviewing data can take years, and—in the context of the assessment cycle—these processes happen before changes to the learning environment. This multiyear process stands in contrast to oft-employed yearly reporting cycle for assessment (Lyons & Polychronopolous, 2018). Faculty, then, are operating within a structure that may explicitly prevent them from the sort of long-term reflection, inquiry, and targeted refinement that successful improvement efforts require.

We agree that the three areas referenced are indeed obstacles to improvement. Nevertheless, we posit that there is another more fundamental obstacle to improvement: Higher educators, administrators, and assessment professionals do not know how to improve student learning *at scale*.

Here, the first author will come clean. I have a PhD in assessment and measurement, and it wasn't until I was a dozen years into the profession that I came to grips with the fact that while my work may have helped demonstrate what learning was happening, it did not actually improve learning at my institution (at least, I had no evidence that it had).

The sobering epiphany prompted action. A team of graduate students and I investigated the literature (Smith et al., 2015). There was little in the way of good strategies for improving student learning at scale. We examined the most popular assessment books, rubrics used by universities to evaluate assessment practice (known as meta-assessment rubrics), and the standards of six regional accreditors. Even though most of these resources referenced the terms *learning* and *improvement*, few mentioned the necessity of reassessment in evidencing improvement. Even fewer gave tangible advice for integrating curriculum and pedagogy into an improvement model at scale.

In short, these references did not provide enough detail to guide learning improvement efforts.

Around the same time, we began experimenting with how to actually improve learning at the academic program level. As opposed to speculating what improvement might look like or analyzing the obstacles, we dove into the machinery of programs. Perhaps from the inside we could figure out how to make improvement work. But somewhere along the way, we realized that the learning improvement problem could not be solved by methodologically minded assessment experts toiling away on their own. We began partnering with our campus's faculty development office and willing faculty partners. As doctoral programs tend to do, we threw dissertations at the problem (e.g., Smith, 2017). We consulted with upper administration. In other words, we were getting smarter and integrating our efforts. Since 2013, we have had success with several academic programs seeking to improve student learning. And, importantly, we believe we now have a deeper understanding of what it takes to achieve improvement and what barriers stand in the way of success.

We weren't the only group examining assessment's role in improvement. The National Institute of Learning Outcomes Assessment (NILOA) profiled nine institutions with a strong track record of using assessment results (Baker et al., 2012). All nine made logical changes to the learning environment informed by assessment results. Good (2015) found that two of the nine institutional examples explicitly referenced better performance of students upon reassessment (i.e., *improvement* as defined in this book): Capella University and Carnegie Mellon University. More recently, the Learning Improvement Community (n.d.) website has collected and profiled learning improvement stories. As of this writing, programs from five institutions have been profiled: University of Alabama, University of Hawai'i at Mānoa, James Madison University, Waubonsee Community College, and York College of Pennsylvania.

While these examples give hope that improvement at scale can be achieved, their scarcity begs the question: Why is improvement so difficult to achieve? The biggest problem—and most exciting opportunity—we see is a lack of coherent strategy for how to improve learning at scale. Kristen Smith (2017) spoke eloquently about the issue, opening her dissertation by arguing that higher education today is in a similar position to Sony at the turn of the millennium. At the time, Sony owned the rights to a huge music catalog, sold products that played digital music, and controlled a large market share of both areas. Nevertheless, Sony failed to successfully integrate these parts of their company. Simultaneously, another company with a much weaker market position began developing a product that seamlessly integrated the music-technology experience: Apple's iPod. The rest is history.

Similarly, today's colleges have access to expertise in content areas (faculty), instructional design (faculty developers), student learning evaluation (assessment experts), and learning sciences (educational researchers and cognitive scientists). Nevertheless, colleges are mishandling these "educational parts" much like Sony mishandled its music and technology. As currently configured, the whole of higher education's learning system is no better than the sum of its parts.

From our vantage point, we—assessment professionals—were approaching the lack-of-improvement problem from the assessment perspective. We thought the most important question was how to better use assessment results for improvement. This question is not a bad one, but it is far too narrow. We were asking a question about an isolated part, hoping the answer would solve a system-sized problem.

Assessment professionals' failure to ask (and answer) the right questions has had insidious consequences. The question we focused on—how to better use assessment results for improvement—implies that the learning improvement problem would be solved by making assessment results more accurate and useful. Indeed, many of us in the assessment community (including ourselves) conceptualized the lack-of-improvement problem as a methodological issue. If we could only increase the validity of assessment claims; if we could only make the results easier for faculty to digest; if only the results provided diagnostic feedback.

Make no mistake, we *do* need high-quality assessment practices in order to support learning improvement efforts. But good assessment is merely a necessary condition for improvement, not a sufficient one.

Of course, assessment is not the only "part" that has viewed the improvement system too narrowly. Other necessary—but, alone, insufficient—questions include the following:

- How can faculty work together to improve student learning?
- How can administrators such as department heads, deans, provosts, and presidents help faculty prepare for improvement?
- How can faculty development opportunities be used to support improvement efforts?
- What changes in the learning environment (i.e., learning interventions) have been shown to reliably move the needle on student learning?
- How can institutional and accreditation policy support learning improvement?

All of these questions must be addressed within the context of a larger question: How do we build more effective learning systems to positively affect student learning at scale? This question subsumes the others, and the search for its answer forms the basis of this book. We endeavor to help faculty and administrators reconfigure their educational parts to create more effective learning environments, which in turn will facilitate improved student learning at scale.

The Structure of This Book

This book provides practical strategies for learning improvement, enabling faculty to collaborate, and integrating leadership, social dynamics, curriculum, pedagogy, assessment, and faculty development.

Chapters 2 and 3 illustrate the gestalt of our learning improvement strategy. In chapter 2 we tell a program-level improvement story from the perspective of a faculty member. We follow her inspiring story as she and her colleagues

- identify a concern with students' writing;
- build a coalition of colleagues who also want to improve writing at the program level;
- create a vision of what good writing looks like;
- examine the current learning environment, including current student performance and alignment between the current learning environment and the vision;
- design a new learning environment at the program level;
- implement the new learning system; and
- assess and determine that the team's efforts caused statistically and practically significant improvement in students' writing abilities.

Chapter 3 inverts chapter 2. We begin from the reassess stage and work our way back to the individual faculty member first pondering whether they can do something to impact students' writing skills. We peel back each layer of the process and imagine how learning improvement efforts might be thwarted at each stage. Often, we learn as much about a system by examining its failures as we do when studying its ideal form. For example, imagine that the faculty do not reassess students after an effective intervention has been implemented. Even if learning improvement occurs, there will be no data to verify the story. The learning improvement process is unforgiving. One large misstep, at any point, could neutralize the entire effort.

Chapters 4 through 9 dig deeper into the learning improvement steps introduced in chapters 2 and 3. Each chapter provides strategies to help higher educators climb each step successfully. Chapter 10 paints a picture of what higher education could look like in 2041 if learning improvement were embraced. And, finally, chapter 11 describes what you can do to support the movement.

The suggestions provided in this book for learning improvement at scale are not easy. They require leadership, expertise, and persistence. We ask you, the reader, to apply a simple litmus test when evaluating whether you will embrace these concepts: Will your students be better off if you do?

Exercises

At the end of each chapter in Part One we provide exercises intended to increase your facility with the concepts covered therein. The exercises can be completed by you alone but may be more useful (and fun) if worked through by a small team. The following exercises pertain to chapter 1:

1. This book is about learning improvement at scale. What is meant by each one of these terms?
   a. Learning
   b. Improvement
   c. At scale
2. A basic example of learning improvement was provided via biology students' ability to identify bones. Create a similarly short, hypothetical example of learning improvement situated in a program with which you are familiar.
3. What is real-time assessment? How does this approach differ from a learning improvement at-scale approach?
   a. In what situations is real-time assessment appropriate?
   b. In what situations is learning improvement at scale appropriate?
4. Provide three reasons why learning improvement at scale is important.
5. Provide three reasons why learning improvement at scale is rare in higher education.
6. In the past, some assessment professionals conceptualized learning improvement too narrowly, viewing it primarily as a matter of using assessment results better. In addition to using assessment results, what other factors should be considered for learning improvement at scale?

WHAT COULD LEARNING IMPROVEMENT LOOK LIKE IN HIGHER EDUCATION?

Through the perspective of faculty protagonist, Xela, chapter 2 provides a hypothetical account of learning improvement at scale. Xela and colleagues successfully navigate each step of the process from testing the collective will to improve to reassessment. Chapter 2, though lengthy, serves as an important touchstone for the concepts covered in chapters 3 through 9, where parts of Xela's story are referenced and further developed. Finally, we note that Xela's story, situated in a psychology program, is only one example of learning improvement at scale. Programs can be bigger or smaller or be situated in a different discipline such as STEM, education, the arts, or the humanities. The principles highlighted by the Xela example are applicable to virtually any program, in any discipline.

Noticing the Problem

"Call me ASAP. One of your graduates applied for a job. FYI, her email is xxPsychologyBootyxx@gmail.com." The text was from Xela's friend Matt, a high-level manager at a data management company, and a member of the Psychology Department's advisory board. The student's job application was the laughingstock of a hiring committee. Matt was kind enough to give her this feedback, but Xela was frustrated. How could a student be so careless? Sure, over her 20 years in the department she had seen several ridiculous email handles. Two years ago, a student in her department used his personal email—Freudshemorrhoids@yahoo.com—to contact a journal editor. The secretary of the psychology club once used Jungthing4U@gmail.com on a school flyer. At least those two were clever. But xxPsychologyBootyxx@gmail.com?

Nothing redeeming at all. Xela knew this particular student to be (otherwise) quite talented. What a thoughtless way to blow a career opportunity.

Still seething, something clicked in Xela's mind. The problem was far bigger than the email handles. She had so frequently seen students communicate in ways that were mismatched to or inappropriate for their audiences that she almost didn't notice it anymore. She jotted down the examples that came to mind most quickly. Thankfully, few were as egregious or embarrassing as this one, but they were nonetheless problematic.

Earlier that semester, a state legislator had stopped by the department's research fair to look at posters and chat with a few students. When Xela asked the representative what she thought of the students' presentations, the representative shrugged. "Most of it was way over my head, but the students seemed excited." This was not the response Xela was hoping for. She had told the students their posters and discussions needed to be accessible to an educated but nontechnical audience, and she was disappointed that her guidance had clearly been ignored. Over all of the years she had overseen the research fair, many other brilliant visitors from outside of the university had stopped by. Guests without a social science background regularly made remarks similar to that of the lawmaker.

The previous year, she had taught her usual introductory research methods course. Throughout the semester, students wrote portions of an American Psychological Association (APA)–style research paper. They received feedback on each portion, made revisions, and then turned in a full-length version of the paper for their final project. Although some students grasped the feel and tone of a scientific research paper, most students missed the mark. One student handed in what appeared, at first, to be a piece of fiction—dialogue and all—for his introduction section. She had provided numerous examples of research papers to reference during their writing process, so why had she received such off-the-wall documents?

The issue seemed to be that students were consistently struggling to match their writing to the situation. They weren't considering the audience to whom they wrote, the purpose of the writing, or the situation in which the written work would be read. This misalignment between writing and context manifested in several different ways, but it was showing up in courses across the curriculum, graduate school applications, communication between students and faculty members, and students' research experiences.

Xela faced a difficult decision. The easy thing to do would be to let this issue go. She was busy with her 3/3 teaching load, her responsibilities as the psychology program's assessment coordinator, and her goal of publishing two scholarly articles per year. But she cared deeply about her students. She knew that students' communication abilities could be the deciding factor in whether a sharp, promising graduate has a number of job offers or no call-backs at all. She'd recently read an article that identified poor writing as a "kiss of death" in the graduate school application process (Appleby & Appleby, 2006, p. 19). The more she thought about it, the more she believed that the department should prioritize helping students communicate effectively in various contexts.

As serious as the problem was, she knew that faculty development could have a huge influence over the learning environment that students experience. Several years ago, when Xela was a junior faculty member, she participated in a series of faculty development workshops. Some were hosted by her home institution and others took place at conferences. She particularly enjoyed the course-redesign workshops where she was pushed to think about the SLOs that were important and then supported in using backward design to build the course from that perspective. Indeed, students in her introductory psychological statistics course seemed to be much stronger in their results interpretation skills after she went through the redesign process with that course.

Despite wanting to take matters into her own hands, she knew that only a small fraction of the students in the department took her classes. The six course sections she taught most years made up just over 2% of the 250 course sections annually taught by the department's 50 instructors. Xela estimated that fewer than a quarter of the university's psychology students ever took a course with her. That meant that no matter how effective Xela became at teaching audience-aligned writing, most students would still be unaffected by her efforts. Even if every student she taught was able to master these skills, most of her department's students would see no difference at all. To help all students, this issue needed to be more than just *her* priority. It needed to be a priority for the entire program.

Xela remembered an information session she had attended earlier in the year. Her university offered "Learning Improvement at Scale" (LIS) support to a handful of programs each year. While traditional course redesign workshops (e.g., the one she had completed years before) supported individual faculty in working on individual classes, this program was different. It specifically targeted learning improvement initiatives at the program level and beyond, requiring a group of faculty members to work together in order to improve student learning on a larger scale.

She recalled that an early part of the process involved determining the program's level of faculty and administrative support. Here, fortunately, Xela was well positioned. She could easily recall several conversations among faculty members on issues related to students' difficulties communicating to a particular audience or context. The topic and its importance would not be a surprise to her colleagues. Further, the faculty in the department had good relationships with each other. For the most part, faculty treated each other well, talked through issues, and collaborated effectively on projects.

Last, Xela was well respected. She knew most of her colleagues and had good relationships with them. Flipping through her vita, she identified about 20 faculty members in the department with whom she had collaborated on various projects over the years. She was known as someone who got the job done on time, with high quality, and with minimal disruption. She didn't ask much from her colleagues, but when she requested their help, most would quickly come to her side. Finally, Xela had a good relationship with the department head. On more than one occasion, Xela had helped the department head work through delicate situations with upper administration. She figured that, given the right approach, she could convince her colleagues that this problem was worth solving.

Testing the Collective Will to Improve

With this context in mind, Xela began building a coalition. The first person she approached was Rusty. Rusty had been in the department a few years longer than Xela. He cared deeply about student learning, but he was known to be temperamental. If he liked something the department was doing, he would be their loudest cheerleader. If he didn't like something, he was their fiercest critic. Either way, Rusty's only volume was loud. But because of his long history in the department and his devotion to his students, he tended to have a strong influence over many faculty members. At his best, he was persuasive, motivating, and hard-working. Xela and Rusty had published together and cotaught a handful of courses and, fortunately, found that their styles complemented one another.

Xela and Rusty sat down together. Xela told Rusty about the embarrassing email address and her larger realization that psychology students, even the best ones, may not have the skills to tailor their communication appropriately to audiences. Rusty laughed at the email handle and shared some of his own outrageous examples. As they talked, Rusty became convinced of the importance of a new, program-wide push for improving students' communication skills. In particular, he thought that they should focus on students' ability to write appropriately in various contexts. Communication was just too big of a topic, he argued, and a subset of writing skills seemed to be a reasonable place to start. Xela agreed. It seemed impossible that students would be able to avoid writing after they graduated, no matter which career or educational path they pursued. Strong writing skills would undoubtedly set their students apart. By the end of the meeting, Rusty had agreed to cochampion the effort with Xela.

With the beginnings of a core team established, Rusty and Xela started reviewing the literature. Rusty focused on the general principles of learning science and cognition that might inform their process, while Xela focused on the scholarship of teaching and learning in psychology. The first article Rusty found described the surprisingly weak relationship between cognitive psychology and college instruction (Matlin, 2002). The article provided a list of articles that laid out frameworks, concepts, and effective practices from the cognitive psychology literature that could be used to inform more effective teaching. Rusty quickly narrowed in on the idea of metacognition. Effective writing requires reflection, planning, and intentional decisions about how the writer's approach fits the demands of the audience and style of writing (Sitko, 1998). He wondered: What were the benefits of increased self-reflection in the writing process? And how could metacognition be increased? Xela, in contrast, found a number of articles about teaching writing in undergraduate psychology programs. While none seemed to specifically discuss teaching alignment between context and writing style, she found a wealth of information about different approaches to teaching writing in psychology courses. In particular, she focused on interventions that required students to dissect the elements of writing through textual analyses, revision processes, and self-reflections. It seemed that students tended to write better when they learned how writing could be deconstructed and analyzed. And wasn't that similar to metacognition?

Xela and Rusty were savvy regarding office politics and organizational communication. They knew that most department heads did not like to be blindsided by new initiatives. Further, they knew that without the support of the department head, any program-level initiative would be dead on arrival. So, before they started talking to other faculty, they reached out to Maria. They told her that they were in the initial stages of considering a department-wide learning improvement project and asked whether she would be willing to provide input and support. The three set up a meeting to discuss the idea further.

Maria had been department head for 4 years. She was a no-nonsense leader but generally considered fair-minded. She had been in the role long enough to be cautious about ideas that necessitated sweeping departmental changes. She had seen a couple examples herself of initiatives that crashed and burned and had heard countless horror stories from other department heads. That said, Maria did consider learning a priority. How could it not be? She viewed the process of graduating students who are prepared for life after college as the single most important job of her unit. Furthermore, she trusted

Xela and Rusty. They were hard-working, trustworthy faculty members who were committed to doing right by students and their colleagues. She would at least listen to what they had to say, but she would reserve judgment until hearing more.

When Maria met with Xela and Rusty, they explained that they had a seed for an initiative that could greatly benefit students. But, before spending too much time and energy refining the idea, they wanted to consult with Maria to vet ideas, get feedback, strategize, and gauge Maria's level of support. Rusty relayed their stories about inappropriate communication, starting with the ridiculous email handles. Based on the comments they had heard from their colleagues over the years, they felt the written communication problems were wide-reaching. They also explained that the university had resources to support program-level learning improvement through the LIS program.

Accessing these university resources was not a given. The psychology program would need to make a compelling case that their project was worth investment; sound learning outcomes and a tenable strategy for improvement needed to be demonstrated. They would need to persuade the university that faculty in the department were willing to work as a team to affect all students in the program. They needed to prove that the faculty who would be responsible for implementing the interventions were willing to do so. Otherwise, the improvement project would not be fully implemented across the program, and not all students would benefit from their efforts.

Maria listened, appreciating Xela and Rusty's preparedness. She was surprised that the university actually had resources to support learning improvement at the program level. Still, she had questions.

Maria: Xela, you're the assessment coordinator. Do we have any assessment data suggesting this area needs to be improved?

Xela: Only tangential information. We use a common rubric to evaluate students' writing in two courses: our introductory research methodology course and the capstone course. But the assignments used in those courses only ask for one very specific type of writing. The rubric can give us some information about the quality of the writing, but we don't test students' ability to adjust their styles to varying contexts. We don't teach these skills, either.

Maria: Isn't that a problem? Shouldn't we collect data first to see if we need to improve writing in various contexts?

Xela: The LIS process acknowledges that often what we want to improve hasn't been well defined yet, and that can raise some questions. In our case, we haven't articulated what we mean by "well-aligned written communication," we haven't assessed it, and as far as I can tell we don't teach it in any systematic way. Fortunately, the LIS process encourages programs in situations like ours to submit proposals. Right now, we have to lay out the problem, show our learning area is important for students, and show that our faculty are committed to working on the effort. As the LIS folks say, the goal is learning improvement from the outset. If we were to be accepted, our team would work alongside professionals in assessment and faculty development to do a few things. First, we'd articulate exactly what we mean by "well-aligned written communication" in order to create a common vision for improvement. Then, we'd evaluate how the psychology program is currently teaching aligned writing skills, and we'd figure out a way to measure how well students are doing in this area right now. Next, we'd create a plan for changing the learning system to teach aligned writing skills more effectively. They would support us in implementing that new learning system, and then we'd assess students again to see if they are better writers under that future curriculum than our students are right now.

Maria: That sounds like a lot of support. You mentioned that we need to demonstrate that our people are on board. Fifty faculty members teach in our program. I assume most of them will be at least somewhat interested in such an initiative. But there are a few faculty members who are going to oppose. How are you planning to deal with their opposition?

Xela: Great question. One of the misconceptions of a program-level learning improvement effort is that all program faculty must be on board. By "program-level," they mean that all students are affected, not that all faculty have to participate. So, for example, if we were to make significant changes to PSYC 202, PSYC 302, and PSYC 402—all required courses in the program—only the 15 faculty members teaching those three courses would need to be on board. Those 15 faculty could collectively change the learning environment that affects all students.

Maria: In that case, we should think about which courses might be logical places for interventions, and then consider which faculty would likely be on board.

Xela: Exactly. There are several courses where proper writing alignment does not fit conceptually. So, faculty members teaching those courses would not participate. And, there are other courses where the conceptual fit might be good, but we know the faculty teaching those courses probably wouldn't be supportive of this effort. So, those courses would likely be tossed out. Nevertheless, we likely have enough courses where a new intervention makes sense *and* the faculty will be supportive and collaborative.

Maria: How long does a project like this take?

Rusty: Often, it takes 3 or 4 years. We want to do this process right. We'll spend the 1st year trying to define what exactly we mean by *aligned written communication* and collecting baseline data on our outgoing seniors to determine their proficiency (which means we'll also need to develop an assessment approach). The 2nd year will be spent forming the strategy. We'll figure out what changes in the learning environment need to occur and how to ensure that all faculty in the intervention pathway are prepared to make these changes. The next couple years are spent on implementation and reassessment to see if the new curriculum is effective.

Maria: Sounds like a big commitment.

Rusty: Absolutely. Learning improvement at this scale is rare in higher education. There are no quick and easy fixes to important problems. The LIS program recognizes this. It's not an easy process, but it has been proven effective in other programs.

Xela: I should add that the greatest time commitment, above and beyond what faculty would normally do, is in the first 2 years. That's when we have to develop the strategy, and then the involved faculty would need to participate in faculty development to redesign the relevant parts of their courses. The next couple of years constitute delivering the materials the faculty have already created and then waiting until students have completed the redesigned courses so that we can reassess their learning.

Maria: Thanks to you both for this information. It seems like the next step is getting the word out to our colleagues about this proposal and asking them if they would be interested.

Xela: Yes. And, Maria, we'd appreciate your advice regarding how to start getting feedback.

Maria: It seems to me that we should first identify those courses that might be reasonable candidates for involvement. From there, figure out which of those courses might have close to full participation from the faculty. Then, when we announce the effort, we can be transparent. Have you given much thought regarding which courses might be reasonable?

Rusty: Xela and I have some thoughts. Out of the eight courses that are required for all psychology majors, five of them seem to be reasonable conceptual fits.

Maria: Excellent. I'll give you 30 minutes at the next department meeting to pitch the idea. Then, if the group seems relatively interested, I'll suggest that each of the five prospective course teams meet with the two of you individually. That way they can determine if the project is a good match for them, especially considering the time commitment. Is there any information you'd like for me to send out to faculty prior to the department meeting?

Xela: Great plan. We'll prepare for the department meeting. The LIS initiative handout we discussed earlier would be useful for our colleagues to read ahead of time. Would you mind sending that out?

Maria: I'd be happy to.

Two weeks later, at the department meeting, Maria announced that the department was considering applying for a LIS project. She stressed to her colleagues that the proposal's submission was dependent on the faculty's willingness to participate. "Let me make it clear," she said, "this is not something our department is required to do, but I encourage you to think carefully about this. If you are willing to jump on board, so am I." Maria turned the meeting over to Xela and Rusty.

They opened by sharing the story about the email address. After the exasperated laughter died down, they gave other examples where students sent embarrassingly informal emails to faculty or wrote papers that were far too casual (or too technical) for the audience. The group then spent the next 15 minutes sharing their own examples with each other. The room was abuzz. There was not a single faculty member who hadn't experienced egregiously misaligned writing assignments from their students.

At this point, Rusty took the floor. "There are two questions that are worthy to consider at this point," he said. "First, is this problem important enough for us to pursue? Then, even if we do think it's worthwhile, do we have the capacity to do it?" Rusty wanted to get a further read on the room. "What's the plus side of taking on the initiative?"

Several faculty members spoke. One said, "Did you hear the buzz a few minutes ago when you asked us to share examples? Obviously, you've struck a nerve." Another faculty member piped up and said, "Yeah, I get it. A graduate's ability to align communication could factor into getting a job or getting promoted. Our program looks bad if our students can't get jobs or can't get into graduate school because they don't know how to write appropriately."

Returning to his second question, Rusty explained that the LIS project came with some support, such as occasional course releases for initiative leaders and summer stipends. This would mean that faculty could use the summer to evaluate student work to get a sense of where students were weak and where they were strong. Additionally, they may use the time to strategize and design their new curriculum. Rusty admitted that a project like this often takes 3 to 4 years from start to finish, even with the resources for summer work. And, while the university provided some support, the will to achieve the project ultimately rested with them. Sensing that the time to voice hesitation had arrived, hands shot up:

P.T. Buck: Is it really our responsibility to teach students how to write appropriately? Shouldn't they have learned how to write in their general education courses?

Tim Auvan: This is interesting and all. But to be frank, it just isn't as important to me as my research. I'm going up for tenure in 2 years, and I can't afford distractions.

S. Tatus Quo: My classes are packed with material as it is. I already have high expectations for my students. How am I supposed to add something new on top of that?

Matthew Sela: I've been in this program for 35 years. I've been watching fad projects like these come and go since you were a twinkle in your parents' eyes. I wasn't interested then, and I'm certainly not interested now.

Xela listened carefully to her colleagues' concerns. "Thank you for raising these issues. Maybe you've been burned in the past by poorly planned initiatives, or maybe you've got too many other tasks on your plate, or maybe you think this is outside the scope of our responsibility here. In any case, it's a decision that each of you have to make whether the potential merits of this project outweigh the costs."

Maria chimed in: "If we are going to do this as a department, we need the faculty from at least two courses to join us. It would be great if we had more. There's no easy fix to a problem like this. Xela, Rusty, and I looked over the eight courses that are required of all our students and five seemed to be reasonable fits for this intervention. I'd like the lead faculty of each of these teams to meet with Xela and Rusty. Let me know if you would be interested in partnering. I encourage you to reach out to Xela and Rusty if you have questions. Send me a decision on your team's willingness to participate by the end of the month."

When the end of the month arrived, Maria called Xela and Rusty into her office. "It looks like all the faculty members in three courses are on board," she told them "You have my permission to submit a LIS proposal. Good luck. This would be good for the department."

The three courses with full support were as follows:

- PSYC 201—an introductory-level research methods course (10 sections taught annually; five instructors teach two sections apiece)
- PSYC 310—a course on careers in psychology usually taken during students' junior year (10 sections taught annually; five instructors teach two sections apiece)
- PSYC 495—the senior-year capstone course (15 sections taught annually; five instructors teach three sections apiece)

Xela and Rusty were pleased with the final course selection: Xela taught the research methods course each semester, and Rusty taught the capstone course. They would not only be working to lead the learning improvement process but also participating as instructors. Xela and Rusty created a diagram (see Figure 2.1) displaying these courses, sections, and instructors visually. First, they created a rectangle containing the name of each instructor. They grouped the rectangles by course. Second, they added the courses each person was responsible for teaching (e.g., Jessica taught sections 1 and 2 of PSYC 201, so her box listed "201.01" and "201.02"). They noticed that none of the instructors overlapped across the three courses, meaning that there were 15 people who would need to change their courses to meet the new objectives. Xela and Rusty got to work on the proposal (see Appendix B).

LIS

Two months later, the department received the good news. They had been awarded one of the two new LIS projects for the year. The project would partner them with two learning improvement coaches: an expert in faculty development and an expert in assessment. Xela and Rusty would each receive a summer stipend for leading the learning improvement initiative, and a small number of course releases would be provided to make time for faculty development related to the initiative.

Xela and Rusty began meeting regularly with their coaches. Ida had served as a writing faculty member for 10 years and for the past 7 had also worked closely with the faculty development office, serving as an "associate" several times. She'd facilitated course redesign workshops and had

Figure 2.1. Visual representation of instructors, courses, and sections.

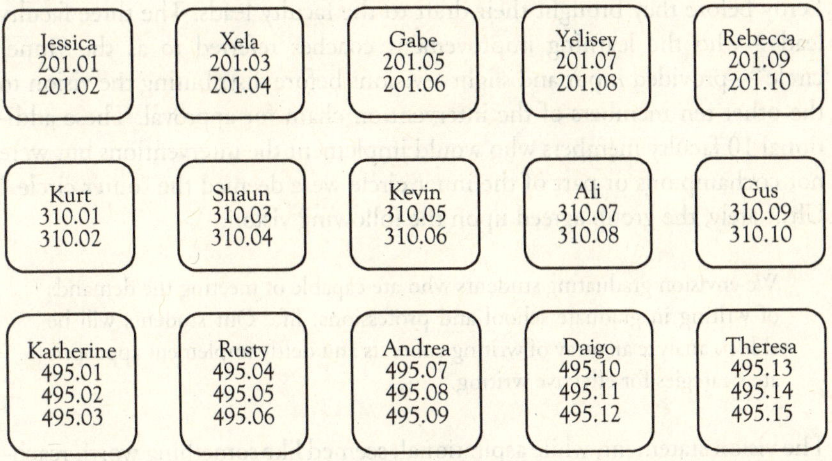

Jessica 201.01 201.02	Xela 201.03 201.04	Gabe 201.05 201.06	Yelisey 201.07 201.08	Rebecca 201.09 201.10
Kurt 310.01 310.02	Shaun 310.03 310.04	Kevin 310.05 310.06	Ali 310.07 310.08	Gus 310.09 310.10
Katherine 495.01 495.02 495.03	Rusty 495.04 495.05 495.06	Andrea 495.07 495.08 495.09	Daigo 495.10 495.11 495.12	Theresa 495.13 495.14 495.15

previous consultation experience with faculty who wanted to improve their students' writing. She was a double threat: She could help Xela and Rusty think through the problems they faced with student writing, and she also could help them think through curriculum revision and faculty development.

Their other coach, Leroy, worked in the university assessment office. Leroy's specialty was instrument design. He'd worked alongside experts in many fields to design a variety of assessments. He enjoyed listening to stakeholders and selecting or developing tests that best fit their needs. Ida and Leroy had both attended a learning improvement academy offered by leaders in learning improvement at another institution.

In their first meeting, Ida and Leroy congratulated Xela and Rusty on their successful learning improvement application. In particular, they noted that the Psychology Department's case had been compelling because it clearly outlined *why* the targeted learning area was important for students and it demonstrated that all faculty in the "intervention chain"—their word for all of the faculty who would be involved with the project—were on board. These elements formed a promising foundation for the next few years of work.

Developing a Vision

Their first task was to develop a common vision of the improvement effort. What would it look like if the improvement initiative were successful? The goal was to draft a guiding statement that could be revised by the three faculty leads for the affected courses and agreed on by all 12 of the additional faculty members in the intervention chain.

Xela and Rusty spent a few weeks workshopping the vision with Ida and Leroy before they brought their draft to the faculty leads. The three faculty leads—who the learning improvement coaches referred to as the "inner circle"—provided input and slight revisions before distributing the vision to the other ten members of the intervention chain for approval. These additional 10 faculty members who would implement the interventions but were not cochampions or part of the inner circle were deemed the "outer circle." Ultimately, the group agreed upon the following vision:

> We envision graduating students who are capable of meeting the demands of writing in graduate school and professional life. Our students will be able to analyze an array of writing contexts and deftly implement appropriate strategies for effective writing.

The vision statement, while aspirational, seemed like something worth reaching for. The faculty dreamed of students who did not grumble when faced with a writing assignment, who felt ownership over their writing processes, and who ultimately did not view writing as a barrier to their educational and professional success.

Establish SLOs

With the vision statement established, it was time to create new SLOs. Xela and Rusty drafted the outcomes with Ida and Leroy, refined them with the inner circle, and sought final approval from the members of the outer circle.

The most contentious part of the conversation was scope. Even with the vision statement in mind, one faculty member wanted to write broad, sweeping SLOs to address writing generally. Others wished to focus on improving students' writing skills on writing a research report. Xela and Rusty carefully listened to these perspectives and reminded everyone that learning improvement projects are typically relatively narrow, especially the first one a program undertakes. And, everyone had agreed that audience misalignment was a major concern. Perhaps if they could conquer this problem then they could focus on other aspects of writing in a future effort.

By the end of the review process, the full team had settled on three SLOs:

Upon graduating from the psychology program, students will do the following:

1. Recognize the elements of a writing context that influence appropriate choice of writing strategy.

2. Explain the reasons for differences among written communication styles relevant to psychological research, scientific communication, and professional workplaces.
3. Demonstrate the ability to write about the same content for a number of different audiences, purposes, and occasions.

The process of refining the learning outcomes was important for several reasons. First, all faculty members involved in the intervention chain needed to have a clear understanding of what it would look like for their students to achieve the intended results of the initiative. Second, the process allowed the people participating in the initiative to coconstruct and document their goals for student learning. Third, the outcomes formed the basis for the interventions and assessment approaches that would soon need to be designed.

Where Are We Now?

The process of drafting the outcomes sparked uncomfortable conversations among the members of the intervention chain. "I don't teach this stuff," a new faculty member mumbled at the end of one meeting. "Why didn't anyone tell me that I should be covering these things? I thought they would just pick these things up like I did when I was in school."

"I don't teach it either," one of his colleagues reassured him. "That's why we're doing this."

Surely enough, when it came time to evaluate the current curriculum and identify where these outcomes were currently being taught, the team found that none of the faculty were teaching in a way that supported the new outcomes. Only one faculty member mentioned devoting any class time to discussing the difference between writing a research report and writing about psychological topics in other contexts. Most of the instructors assigned writing projects to students, but they rarely spoke explicitly about how the kinds of writing they expected students to produce differed from each other. Moreover, the feedback they provided to students often seemed to frustrate both student and instructor. Invariably, instructors would tell students that they were not following proper style conventions. Students would respond by asking *what* those style conventions were. Exasperated, the instructors would grumble to each other about students these days just wanting a checklist, an easy way out, without having to think their way through a problem.

The conversations during this process indicated that each faculty member figured that students would pick up knowledge about appropriate writing from reading the varied works assigned to them throughout their time in the major. This assumption was held by most everyone on the team. Even Rusty and Xela knew that prior to beginning the LIS application process they had held the same belief. Clearly, though, students were not extracting this information from their coursework. Something needed to change.

Ida and Leroy offered some reassurance. "The root of this process is figuring out what's wrong with the current curriculum so that we can make things better," said Ida at the end of a particularly difficult workshop session. "We would never see these areas of misfit if we hadn't started looking. We're going to find elements of the curriculum that don't make much sense, and we're going to dig up assumptions about our students that don't hold water. That's part of the process. We just have to make sure we take that discomfort and turn it into action so that the next phase of the curriculum *does* prepare students to meet these outcomes."

The faculty members in the intervention chain knew that not only were they not teaching students how to select and execute appropriate writing strategies, but they also were not formally assessing these skills in their students. Initially, most of the faculty saw no problem with the absence of existing assessment data. After all, hadn't they each been able to recall instances of inappropriate writing from their students? Besides, why would they need to measure something they weren't even teaching? They knew scores would be dismal: wasn't that the whole point of the LIS project?

Leroy, the assessment expert, explained the importance of the baseline measurement in a meeting with all participants in the intervention chain. "Think of the last advertisement you saw for a gym. It probably included pictures of the same person before *and* after joining the gym. They're trying to show you how a person changed as a result of their gym membership. Similarly, we could just go ahead and change the curriculum and measure graduating seniors in 2 years. Let's say we make a rubric to measure appropriate writing skills and we find that those seniors score a 4.3 out of 6, on average, 2 years from now. How can we interpret that number if it's the only data we have? We won't know if a 4.3 represents an improvement if we have nothing to which we can compare. We can't use that information to demonstrate that students then are better than students now if we don't have corresponding information from the curriculum that's already in place."

"Why don't we just test our new students, then?" asked Rebecca, an instructor for the research methods course. "We could create this measure and then give it to all the students next academic year right after they declare the psychology major. Wouldn't that work as a baseline?"

"Actually, that's a bit different," Leroy replied. "That's what we'll refer to as 'pretest' data, and while it can be useful for other purposes, it wouldn't give us the information we need here. When we talk about learning improvement, we're talking about improving learning across an entire academic program, not just within an individual student. If we wanted to know how much a given *student* improves over their time in the program, we'd get that pretest data and compare it to their scores when they graduate from the program. That would tell us how much the student improved since we last measured them. But since we're evaluating the entire program, we need to take a measure of the *program's* effectiveness—which we conceptualize as the skills of seniors graduating from the program—as it stands now so that we can compare that to the program's effectiveness after we tackle this problem and change up the curriculum."

Once the distinction was clear, the team set to work developing a measure of appropriate writing skills. Working with Leroy, Rusty and Xela spent the next few months reviewing similar measures, learning about instrument development, and designing a plan for gathering data from all graduating seniors at the end of the spring semester. In the end, they were able to develop three measures: one multiple-choice test and two performance assessments. The multiple-choice test (designed to measure SLO 1) included 30 items about the stylistic conventions and contextual considerations in a variety of relevant types of writing. The first performance assessment (designed to measure SLO 2) presented students with brief texts and information about the context in which they were written. The students' task was to evaluate and (if necessary) revise the text in order to meet the demands of the writing context. Students were presented with five texts and could earn up to three points for each. The second performance assessment (designed to measure SLO 3) was embedded in the capstone course. Students were given a context and an audience in a brief vignette and then asked to write about their research project for the capstone course in a manner appropriate for the scenario. Students were presented with three texts and could earn up to five points for each.

After months of work with Leroy, the measures were administered to 100 graduating seniors at the end of spring semester. The results (see Table 2.1), while abysmal, were unsurprising.

While presenting the results to the members of the intervention chain, Xela offered a reminder. "We wouldn't be doing this if students had these skills. This affirms that we're looking in the right place. Plus, we can take this information back to the rest of the department as proof that we're doing important, necessary work."

With encouragement from Xela, Rusty, and the LIS team, the rest of the members of the intervention team got to work. If they wanted to see students improve, they would need a solid plan for making changes to their courses.

TABLE 2.1
Year 1 Assessment Data

		Performance Assessments	
	Multiple choice (SLO 1)	Short answer (SLO 2)	Embedded assessment (SLO 3)
SLO covered	1	2	3
Average score for Year 1 seniors	12.5/30	5.6/15	4.2/15

Developing and Implementing Interventions

While Leroy worked with Rusty and Xela to develop and implement the assessment plan, Ida worked with the team to develop interventions for the courses in the intervention chain. Fortunately, the three participating courses were spaced evenly throughout the program. Students always took the research methods course first, as it was a prerequisite for the rest of the courses in the program. Typically, they took the careers in psychology course in the following year, and the capstone course in their final year. Therefore, faculty teaching the careers in psychology and capstone courses would know that students had received some instruction in appropriate writing prior to these courses.

Ida began the intervention development process by guiding Rusty and Xela through a review of the literature on teaching writing in psychology. During this process, they kept a log of ideas for promising additions to the key courses in the intervention chain. In particular, they focused on developing new interventions that were expected to improve students' metacognitive awareness of their writing processes. They found that their program was not alone in noticing students' difficulties deciphering the conventions of written communication in psychology (e.g., Ishak & Salter, 2017). They also learned that metacognitive approaches to teaching writing prioritized helping students understand how the contexts in which they wrote called for different writing approaches, as students are often unable to teach themselves these skills on their own (Sitko, 1998). This meant that their interventions would need to focus on an explicit understanding of writing contexts and the approaches for which they called.

They also identified the development of effective schemas for writing as an important goal of the new curriculum. Schemas ideally contain sets of rules, procedures, and information about a concept (Mastacusa et al., 2011). This might include general information, graphical information, and procedural information. If the schema is well developed, it allows for deep understanding of the concept as well as related concepts. For example, although students might be able to identify disjointed elements of a writing context (e.g., understanding that the intended audience has some degree of background information about the subject area), they might be unable to integrate that information to create and respond to a writing context more holistically. Interventions should, therefore, target the development of complex schemas for various writing contexts.

In their review of the literature, the team found several interventions that could be used in their courses. Concept maps could be used to help students develop complex schemas of the writing process (Mastacusa et al., 2011). Even better, redrafting the same concept map at the beginning and end of a semester would allow students to visualize how much they have developed in their knowledge of a topic while providing them with repeated practice in accessing the relevant concepts. One idea that was particularly exciting to the team was the "cover letter" approach studied by Daniel et al. (2015), which required students to submit a cover letter describing how they incorporated feedback into their writing assignments. The faculty liked the idea of using the writing assignments that already existed in the capstone course—the sections of which were small enough that the instructors could provide a good deal of feedback on students' writing—and adding a component requiring students to reflect on the choices they were making in each draft. As an added bonus, this approach had been found to result in larger score gains from initial drafts and final paper scores than an approach requiring draft submissions without accompanying cover letters (Daniel et al., 2015).

In the process of developing the interventions, differences among the three course teams emerged. The teams responsible for the capstone and careers in psychology courses sought to agree on a clearly defined intervention that all instructors would implement in a near-identical fashion. These instructors were interested in creating a common assignment with a common rubric, creating a set of slides to be used in all course sections, and assigning the same set of readings for the new intervention. On the other end of the specificity spectrum, the research methods team wanted to retain flexibility in their courses. Although they each agreed to add a new unit about scientific communication and two new assignments, they resisted implementing the intervention in lockstep. Instead, they agreed to meet regularly throughout the semester to discuss their approaches to the new unit and new assignments, providing and receiving feedback on their approaches to the problem.

By the end of the semester, the course modification plans were complete. The members of the inner circle created Table 2.2 with input from the instructors in the outer circle. During the semester's last faculty meeting, they

TABLE 2.2
Planned Course Modifications

Course	Course modifications	SLO coverage
PSYC 201: Research Methods	**Intervention A:** Instructors add a new unit about styles of scientific communication (including research articles, "pop science" articles, TED Talks, and posters for academic conferences). In this unit, instructors will discuss the elements of each type of writing, including *why* those elements occur in each type of writing and why they are important to that type of writing. During this unit, students will create concept maps illustrating the relationships between each type of writing and its features and purposes.	SLO 1 SLO 2
	Intervention B: Two new assignments are added that require students to translate between different styles of scientific writing. For example, students might be required to find a peer-reviewed article and rewrite it as a "popscience" article.	SLO 3
PSYC 310: Careers in Psychology	**Intervention C:** Instructors add a new unit on writing for graduate school and job applications. In this section, faculty will teach about the relationships between professional and academic contexts and the résumés, curriculum vitae, cover letters, personal statements, and emails those contexts require. Students will receive samples of varying quality for each type of writing, which they will review and critique as a class.	SLO 1 SLO 2
	Intervention D: Three "workshop days" are added to the course, along with a day preparing students to give and receive feedback on writing. On the workshop days, students pair up to review a specified type of writing (e.g., a cover letter in response to a job posting or résumé) they have drafted. Additionally, two assignments are added for each workshop day. First, students must prepare the piece of draft writing to be reviewed in the workshop. Second, they must revise and resubmit the writing sample after incorporating feedback from the review session.	SLO 3

Course	Course modifications	SLO coverage
PSYC 495: Capstone	**Intervention E:** Instructors add a new unit on identifying effective and ineffective elements of formal scholarly communication. Using examples from peer-reviewed articles, instructors will discuss the importance of providing adequate background knowledge, clear interpretation of statistical results, and adhering to the style conventions of scientific writing.	SLO 1
	Intervention F: The existing assignment for this course (producing a full scholarly research paper) was adapted to focus on the revision process. Previously, students turned in a single version of the research paper at the end of the semester. In the new version of the assignment, students turn in multiple drafts of each section of the paper (abstract, introduction, methods, results, and discussion) at specified points during the semester. In addition to each draft, students provide a cover letter detailing their revisions to previous versions of the draft (if relevant), provide justification for stylistic choices, and identify particular elements of their writing for which they would like to receive feedback.	SLO 3
	Intervention G: A new assignment was created requiring students to write three summaries of their scholarly research paper for three different audiences. Students select three audiences that may be interested in this work, provide a brief explanation of each of the three writing contexts, and submit summaries tailored to each of the three contexts.	SLO 3

presented their plan to the entire psychology department. With the baseline measurement complete and the planned modifications outlined, the faculty in the intervention chain were ready to begin creating new course materials and participating in course redesign workshops over the summer.

Beginning the following fall, faculty implemented the new versions of the three courses. Students wrote slightly more frequently in their classes, but they also received clearer instruction about scientific communication, its quirks, and its uses. Some of the new assignments were immediate successes, while others needed refinements at the end of the first semester. The team responsible for teaching the research methods course met monthly throughout the fall to discuss their individualized approaches to the new unit and new assignments.

Reassessing

Xela and Rusty—with approval from the rest of the department—decided to readminister both the multiple-choice test and the performance assessments each spring for the following 3 years. In the 1st year following the new interventions, all graduating seniors had experienced the new version of the capstone course. A handful of students had also experienced the new careers in psychology course, but none had experienced the new research methods course. Table 2.3 indicates the number of students

TABLE 2.3
Assessment Data and Intervention Implementation From Years 1–4

| | Multiple choice (SLO 1) | Performance Assessments | | Intervention Received |
		Short answer (SLO 2)	Embedded assessment (SLO 3)	
Year 1 (n = 100)	12.5/30	5.6/15	4.2/15	All students experienced the old curriculum
Year 2 (n = 100)	16.8/30	8.9/15	7.3/15	All students experienced new capstone course, some experienced new PSYC 310: Careers in Psychology course
Year 3 (n = 100)	20.2/30	12.8/15	9.9/15	All students experienced new PSYC 495: Capstone course and PSYC 310: Careers in Psychology course, some experienced new PSYC 201: Research Methods course
Year 4 (n = 100)	24.0/30	13.1/15	12.9/15	All students experienced all three new courses

graduating each year and which revised courses the graduating students had experienced. They expected that as more students completed more of the redesigned courses, scores on the assessments would increase. As shown in the table, their expectations matched the data collected over the next 3 years. With each successive year, students' scores on all three measures increased.

These results aligned with the conversations across the department as well: Even the faculty members outside of the intervention chain noticed that their students were writing more clearly, asking better questions when reviewing paper drafts during office hours, and producing better application materials for jobs and graduate programs. In short, the program's new curriculum seemed to be working better than the old one. Student learning had improved across the psychology program.

Celebrating

What an accomplishment! Four years after their initial conversations, students were more thoughtful, effective writers thanks to the changes made by Xela and colleagues.

As department head, Maria wanted to acknowledge her colleagues' hard work. She threw a reception at a local restaurant to honor the participating faculty. She gave a special recognition to Xela and Rusty for being the cochampions and gave them an opportunity to say a few words to their colleagues.

Maria also wanted to make sure that others outside the psychology department knew about the story. Fortunately, the provost made that easy. She had communicated that learning improvement at scale was a division priority and wanted to celebrate and "show off" good examples. Soon, Xela and Rusty found themselves presenting in front of the provost and her leadership team. After the presentation the provost thanked them for their hard work. Turning to the attending deans from other colleges, she asked them to take note of Xela and Rusty's work. "Find the Xelas and Rustys within your own colleges," she requested. "I'd like to see these projects permeate our university within the next 10 years."

Exercises

Xela and her colleagues masterfully navigated improving student learning at scale, from building a coalition through reassessment. This success did not happen by accident. They were strategic along the way. The following exercises ask you to dig into their example.

1. Provide an example in each of the following areas where Xela, Rusty, and their colleagues made effective decisions relative to learning improvement at scale. Identify why each decision was effective.
   a. Building a collective will to improve within a program
   b. Carefully specifying what the learning is that should be improved
   c. Collecting baseline information
   d. Developing or adopting interventions effective at improving the specified learning area
   e. Implementing the interventions in such a way that all students are affected
   f. Reassessing
2. What role did the department head (Maria) play in this initiative? Why was Maria's role important?
3. How did the assessment and faculty development offices support Xela and Rusty's initiative?
4. Think about your home program (or, if your role is not specific to an academic program, think about a program with which you work closely). Every program is different, and it is unlikely that employing the exact process used by Xela and her colleagues would work perfectly in your program. The following questions ask you to compare and contrast your program to Rusty and Xela's.
   a. What strategies did Xela and Rusty use that might work in your program? Why do you think these strategies would be useful in your context?
   b. What strategies did Xela and Rusty use that would not translate well to your program? Why would these strategies be less useful or effective in your context?
5. If you were part of a learning improvement at-scale team, what strengths would you bring to the table? For example, do you have expertise in coalition building or developing assessment instruments? How might these strengths be useful in improving student learning within your program?

DISMANTLING LEARNING IMPROVEMENT

Learning improvement at scale is complex. This chapter examines how each part of the process fits with the whole, and the consequences to improvement when a part is inadequately addressed.

Chapter 2 laid out a learning improvement story, starting with Xela's epiphany that students struggled to adjust their writing to their audience. It culminated with a reassessment showing that students' skills had been transformed thanks to a coordinated faculty effort. Between those two points, Xela, Rusty, and their colleagues made good decision after good decision. And, they were beneficiaries of a pro-improvement culture. The project would not have been successful without strong internal champions, collaborative colleagues within the program, and academic leadership willing to offer the technical expertise and resources to support the faculty team.

The type of learning improvement that Xela and Rusty enjoyed is achievable at any institution. Beware, though, of mistaking "achievable" for "easy." The purpose of chapter 3 is to show the importance of careful planning and execution at each step in the improvement process.

A learning improvement project is, in fact, easy to dismantle. The process is delicate. Any large mistake, or an accumulation of smaller missteps, could undermine the entire enterprise. Many elements—including people—must be in sync for an initiative to result in improved student learning. In other words, there are many necessary conditions for a change initiative to blossom into successful learning improvement at scale. Even if those necessary conditions are in place, enough slippage along the path will render a change initiative fruitless.

To provide hope, we remind readers that many, many complex and unforgiving systems produce their desired results every day. Millions of automobiles take us from one destination to the other, electric grids power entire countries, internet connections enable commerce and communication, and elections gather the political inclinations of millions. Each of these systems requires countless subsystems, the sum of generations of expertise, to work in tandem. Of course, mistakes happen, but more often than not the systems function as intended. So too can learning improvement function effectively in higher education. We just need to understand the elements involved, their necessary connections, and the consequences of missteps in order to design for success.

This chapter will start by dismantling the end of the learning improvement process in the reassessment stage. We will then work our way back to problems that can occur at the beginning of an improvement initiative. Throughout each section, we will assume all prior steps have been completed successfully up to the specified step. So, for example, when we examine reassessment, we imagine the faculty have

- secured colleagues' and administrators' support for the initiative,
- arrived at a common vision of learning,
- explored the current learning environment,
- developed a new learning system, and
- implemented the new system successfully.

Nevertheless, after that string of successes, our protagonists do not reassess their would-be successful improvement effort. This oversight would cause major problems with their ability to demonstrate learning improvement. Any number of issues may arise when a link breaks at other points in a learning improvement initiative. By laying out the potential sources of error in the learning improvement process, we hope to provide a road map for success for future endeavors.

Reassessment

The purpose of this stage is to determine whether all the planning and coordination eventuated into the desired outcome of improved learning at scale. When successful, reassessment is the crowning event of a collective effort.

Recall that in chapter 2 Xela, Rusty, and their colleagues reassessed at the end of the 4th year. They rejoiced when students' skills on the measures of writing significantly and noticeably increased. But a variety of problems could have derailed their efforts, even at this late stage in the process.

First, the department could have halted its improvement efforts prior to reassessment. Imagine that, content with the coordinated change to the learning environment, Xela, Rusty, and their colleagues decided to turn their time and energy to other efforts. Conversations among the faculty indicated that students were better able to choose appropriate writing strategies, and they believed this to be a sufficient demonstration of the intervention's effectiveness. In this case, students' skills *have* improved, but the program has only anecdotal evidence to back the improvement claim. This is a tragic situation, and it's unfortunately common. It's akin to a marathoner running at world record speed, only to find out that the timing mechanism malfunctioned: They would never know that they had broken the record. If a new curriculum results in desired outcomes and no one is around to assess it, does it qualify as an improvement? We would argue it does not.

Alternatively, the department might have conducted reassessment using methods or measurement tools that differed from those used during the initial assessment. From a methodological perspective, reassessment conditions must be kept as similar to the initial assessment as possible. If this is done well, a more compelling case can be made that differences in scores are attributable to the difference in the learning environment from one point to another (rather than to methodological differences between the testing occasions). In layman's terms, we are trying to reduce the methodological noise so we can hear the learning improvement signal as clearly as possible.

To illustrate the point, consider the following types of misalignment:

- *Differences in items between the two assessment occasions.* A mantra in the measurement community, attributed to Albert Beaton and Rebecca Zwick (1990), is relevant here: If you want to measure change, don't change the measure. Imagine if faculty were to revise the instrument between the initial assessment and reassessment. Perhaps they change 75% of the items. When comparing initial assessment scores to the reassessment, it is impossible to untangle the effects of the intervention from the changes made to the measure.
- *Differences in data collection strategies between the two assessment occasions.* Imagine that students in the first cohort were given an hour to complete the test, but students in the second cohort were given 2 hours. Or, perhaps, the test was administered in a classroom for one cohort but was sent to students via email to complete at their leisure in another cohort. Much like the previous example, we would be unable to disentangle differences in the data collection from differences in student performance.
- *Cohort differences.* This last form of misalignment is subtle, but deadly nonetheless. Recall that the initial assessment uses a different group of students than the reassessment. Imagine if the learning improvement

team did nothing to show the equivalence of the cohorts. An astute methodologist could hypothesize that the differences observed between testing occasions may be a result of preexisting differences. Perhaps the seniors in the second cohort entered the program as better writers than those in the previous cohort. In this case, it would be possible that score differences between the cohorts were due to these preexisting skill differences rather than the changes to the learning environment. This particular methodological misalignment can be particularly challenging for small programs and/or programs that have drastically changed their recruiting or admissions practices.

Implementation

The purpose of this stage is to execute the learning improvement plan. This step translates the planned intervention into action, ensuring that all faculty implementers are prepared for and supported in the implementation process.

Recall in chapter 2 that all sections of three different courses served as the intended vehicles for changing the learning environment. In total, 15 faculty members (two cochampions, three faculty leads in the "inner circle," and 12 more in the "outer circle") were responsible for teaching these sections. Those 15 faculty participated in a weeklong course redesign process where they worked on materials in sync with their colleagues. Recall, too, that the intervention step requires a disproportionate amount of time and resources compared to the assess and reassess stages. With its outsize share of the effort required for learning improvement to occur, this step contains several pitfalls.

The first potential problem concerns insufficient faculty development for the targeted SLO. Learning improvement initiatives will generally require faculty to develop new skills, learn new teaching techniques, and reconsider long-standing practices in their classrooms. Imagine if, instead of the weeklong opportunity to transform courses as laid out in the previous chapter, Rusty and Xela had simply handed the members of the intervention chain a series of PowerPoint presentations, exercises, and exams, and tasked their colleagues with using them. No matter how well prepared those materials might be, success is far from guaranteed with this approach for a few reasons.

First, incorporating new materials into an existing course is difficult. If an instructor already has a course established, adding new materials isn't as easy as it sounds. The course was likely "full" of presentations, activities, and assessments before the new materials were presented. Merely shoehorning extra material bloats the course. The ideal strategy is for the faculty member to redesign aspects of their course so that it is more efficient and, hopefully, more effective. These changes may range from slight modifications to major overhauls. In any case, the process requires time and careful attention.

A week structured specifically for this purpose enables faculty members to reconfigure course strategies and begin creating modified or new materials that will be used in their courses.

Additionally, instructors (including the authors) find it difficult to adopt wholesale other faculty members' materials. We each have our own styles, strengths, and preferences. That's not to say faculty are unwilling to collaborate with others on materials. We are just saying that faculty typically don't like to be treated like robots. A healthy balance can be struck.

The second possible implementation misstep is not actually delivering the planned program. Imagine that the newly planned curriculum (recall the course modifications described in chapter 2) is not delivered as intended *or* is not delivered at all. In this case, we have an implementation fidelity problem. Implementation fidelity refers to the degree to which a lesson, activity, program, or curriculum is implemented as planned (this concept will be discussed in greater detail in chapter 8). Perhaps a faculty member announces his departure from the university the week before classes begin and an adjunct has to take over his teaching duties on short notice but receives the old course materials. Perhaps another faculty member runs out of preparation time and decides to jettison the newly developed activities and return to her old course plan. Or, perhaps several faculty members became incensed because they had no opportunity to shape the interventions. Feeling that the interventions were too rigid, they refused to change their courses.

Implementation fidelity (or lack thereof) exists on a continuum. On one pole, every faculty member may deliver the program exactly as intended in every section. On the other side, every faculty member may disregard the improvement plan entirely. If 14 out of 15 faculty are on board and are implementing 90% of the agreed-on plan while one faculty member is only doing 30%, a program will still likely see learning improvement (relatively high fidelity). Toward the other extreme, imagine if only Xela and Rusty implemented the changes at 90% fidelity but the other 13 faculty each delivered 20% or less of the changes. With such low overall fidelity, it is quite possible that the program would not detect learning improvement upon reassessment.

We cannot overemphasize the close relationship between these two potential errors in implementation. That is if faculty are not given the space and time to work on changing their courses to align with the larger improvement initiative, then the probability that they will do so is very low.

Designing the New Learning System: Interventions

The purpose of this stage is to establish a strategy to change the learning environment. Here, the core team consults the literature to find or develop effective strategies for achieving the intended goal. Recall that Xela, Rusty,

Ida, and Leroy worked together for a semester to conceptualize the new learning system. They consulted cognitive psychology research (Rusty's work with metacognition) and research on teaching writing (Xela's readings on the scholarship of teaching and learning in psychology) and shared their expertise with the rest of the faculty in the intervention chain. They regularly reconvened with the faculty members in the intervention chain to share their progress and solicit feedback. They ensured that faculty were active contributors throughout the process. By the end of the semester, they had laid out an empirically informed strategy for modifying the three key courses and had received the blessing of all the faculty involved. But what if less attention had been paid to strategy and coalition building?

Imagine first that the team was unable to agree on a plan for implementing program-level changes. Perhaps the department head, Maria, had made a grand speech urging faculty to work on student writing but provided no further guidance or support. While her intent would be worthy of commendation, her actions would not have been specific or strategic enough to make an appreciable program-wide impact on student learning. Joe might have tried one tactic in his section, Sam another, and Julio still another. Or, perhaps, the request would have become buried in the hectic pace of the semester. We're sure that any reader working in higher education can recount many tales of well-intentioned, exciting initiatives that somehow get lost in the shuffle of the academic year. There would have been little chance of any synchronized alignment within sections of courses or across various courses.

Alternatively, we can consider what might happen if an intervention is based purely on speculation instead of theory and research. This misstep, while problematic, is not necessarily damning. Faculty are smart people. If they come up with a plan that is well orchestrated and faithfully implemented, they may indeed achieve some success. But why reinvent the wheel? For most learning areas, a great deal of research has evaluated the effectiveness of various teaching and learning strategies. Precious time spent on local trial and error could be greatly reduced by first exploring what experts have found through systematic study. Building interventions with the guidance of existing research is an efficient way to find effective strategies while increasing the probability of success.

Where Are We Now?

The purpose of this stage is to investigate the existing learning environment and to inventory current efforts to address the targeted SLO. This step also allows the program to make hypotheses about why the current system is not producing the desired learning outcomes.

Recall that Xela and Rusty, with the help of the inner circle, developed a vision statement and SLOs detailing their hopes for student achievement in writing. The team then met with faculty members to determine whether the outcomes were being addressed by the current curriculum. As a result of this process, three of the faculty discussed that they had mentioned, to some degree, the importance of mastering various genres of writing in their courses. Nevertheless, only a single faculty member required students to spend more than 1 or 2 hours thinking about writing-to-audience fit. Nevertheless, he admitted that his strategy was not as well informed as it could be, and he was willing to modify his efforts to be more in line with the group's new instructional plans.

At this step, problems might stem from devoting too little time to understanding what the program is currently doing to meet the targeted SLO. This is akin to a new administrator demanding change before having any idea of what is currently happening. (This is precisely why many new leaders engage in a listening tour before suggesting or mandating change.)

Understanding the program's existing efforts serves two purposes. First, it communicates interest in what faculty are doing. This is particularly important if the initiative is driven by a person in a leadership position, such as a department head. Second, this process may identify brilliant strategies already in place at the individual classroom level to address the identified outcome. Even though many things will necessarily change as the result of a learning improvement process, digging deep into the existing process might reveal pedagogical gold. If it does, these elements should be examined and potentially magnified. Open discussion about the process also serves to lay bare the system. This is a shame-free period. All involved faculty must come to a common agreement that the existing program is not working as desired. Therefore, this is a good opportunity to take that "before" picture—a snapshot used to reflect on the system as it stands.

The second problem that may occur at this step is skipping baseline data collection. This is a death knell for learning improvement. Recall that the simple model for learning improvement requires three steps: assess, intervene, and reassess. If the first assessment never occurs, then no comparison is possible between the old and new systems. No matter how effective the intervention is, it will be impossible to *evidence* learning improvement.

Another problem with skipping the initial assessment is that important information about student performance is lost. Consider the assessment strategy outlined in the previous chapter. The Psychology Department gathered information about students' knowledge of stylistic conventions and contextual considerations, their ability to revise writing to align with a given context, and their ability to write about complex research topics for different audiences. Suppose faculty found that students' scores on stylistic conventions and contextual considerations were acceptable, but the scores on the revision measure were abysmal. This finding would provide key information to the improvement team: They would need to focus their curricular changes on providing students with more opportunities to write and revise writing in order to meet the needs of varying contexts. A close examination of the initial assessment narrows the scope of the intervention and provides a path forward to faculty who might otherwise be unsure where to begin.

Common Vision

The purpose of this stage is to specify exactly what the program desires its students to know, think, or do in a given learning area. Recall that Xela and Rusty established a vision statement, vetted by the inner circle and later shared with all members of the outer circle that clearly outlined the skills and attitudes students would ideally have upon graduating from the program. This vision statement was then solidified into a set of learning outcomes, which were also vetted by all participants in the improvement effort.

The first mistake that can be made here is defining the vision with little clarity and specificity. For example, consider the following statements:

- We will make students better writers.
- We will make students better critical thinkers.
- We will make students more successful in their future jobs.

These general learning goals are reasonable starting points. They draw attention, and they represent a status to which the department may aspire. But they do not provide a clear, common purpose. The difference between the approach we advocate and these examples is analogous to the difference between an essay title and its thesis statement. Both are useful, but the thesis statement is what clearly defines the purpose and provides a sense of direction. Similarly, vision statements and SLOs provide the guideposts from which a successful learning system is developed.

Another problem that may arise in this step is selecting or designing an assessment instrument that is not closely aligned to the targeted SLO. Great assessment instruments not only tightly correspond with the targeted SLO, but their development can be thought of as a further elaboration and clarification of an SLO. In other words, if we want to know what it looks like to achieve an outcome, we can examine the measurement tool that will be used to capture an estimate of student knowledge or skill. Questions on a multiple-choice test or behavioral descriptions within a rubric are more specific than SLOs. When constructed well, measurement tools can be the clearest elaboration of a learning improvement vision. If time is not spent ensuring this alignment, then considerable damage will occur in the learning improvement process. At worst, if the instrument is chosen or created haphazardly, the resulting data will have no correspondence with students' proficiency. For these reasons, we highly recommend involving an assessment expert throughout any learning improvement process.

Testing the Collective Will to Improve

The purpose of this stage is to build a collective intention among faculty to improve some area of learning, even if that area has yet to be clearly defined. Recall how skillfully Xela set about building a coalition. She first met with her longtime friend and faculty collaborator, Rusty. The pair hashed out initial details and decided to move forward together. They then met with Maria, the department head, who offered her support (and, critically, her administrative clout). They then collaborated with their colleagues and picked up well-positioned partners along the way, ensuring that everyone who committed to the initiative had done so of their own volition.

A great many problem points are possible in this step. First, the people involved in the initial conversations—Rusty, Maria, and even Xela—easily could have decided not to act on the issue at hand. This is understandable: Faculty are busy, problems abound, and we cannot expect everyone to have the time, energy, and desire to fix every problem they encounter. But if learning improvement is to take place, someone (or, more likely, a group of people) must be willing to act. No spark, no learning improvement fire.

Choosing who will light the fire is another critical juncture in the process. Taking on a learning improvement project without cochampions is often a mistake. So, too, is choosing the wrong cochampions. The early stages of coalition building often include unstructured discussions of partly formed ideas with close colleagues. The provision of honest feedback from a trusted colleague is as necessary for idea refinement in learning improvement as it is in any other scholarly pursuit. The cochampion may see connections or opportunities that the other champion overlooks. For example, Rusty was able to garner initial buy-in from several faculty members that Xela could not have done on her own. Without a cochampion who can provide honest feedback, quality suggestions, and tenacious pursuit of the project's goals, the initiative is likely to stall.

Overlooking the importance of administrative buy-in poses another risk. Imagine if Xela and Rusty tried to work with other faculty members without first securing Maria's support. Logistically, Xela and Rusty would have lost opportunities to address large groups of people at the department level. Further, they would likely not have had access to her support and resources. Maria may even have actively shut down the effort if she felt that Rusty and Xela were trying to "work around her." The department head should (rightfully) be involved or at least informed of endeavors that affect a significant portion of people in the unit. In fact, if it were not for Maria's dedication to her faculty, the effort could have fallen apart. Department heads who show similar support demonstrate bravery, flexibility, and trust in their colleagues.

Finally, problems may arise if stakeholders are not consulted from the beginning of the process. Recall that Xela and Rusty met with all the instructors of several courses, and they spent a few minutes talking to all faculty members at the department meeting. If they had delayed communication with their colleagues, faculty members would have felt out of the loop. Perceptions of the initiative may have tilted away from communal ownership and toward top-down imposition.

Putting the Pieces Back Together

Chapter 3 dismantled the successful learning improvement journey, brick by brick, that chapter 2 created. The purpose of chapter 3 was to demonstrate how thoughtful and intentional leaders need to be on such projects. Missteps are costly. You likely already know how quickly communication and logistics can, and do, fall apart when buried under the stress and pressures of higher education.

Do not be discouraged. Obstacles are easier to jump over, sidestep, or plow through once visible. The next six chapters (4–9) are designed to help those who dare to improve. Specifically, we illuminate considerations at each step of the learning improvement process, from which you can build a better learning environment for students, layer by layer. Ultimately, students will be more successful because of your efforts. Specifically, you will learn how to do the following:

- Chapter 4: Build a coalition of improvement collaborators
- Chapter 5: Develop a guiding vision for learning improvement

- Chapter 6: Collect baseline data on student performance and environmental conditions
- Chapter 7: Select and/or create evidence-based interventions
- Chapter 8: Implement the interventions, at scale, with fidelity
- Chapter 9: Reassess to determine the extent to which improvement occurred

Exercises

Learning improvement at scale is fragile. As mentioned in this chapter, any large mistake, or an accumulation of smaller missteps, could undermine the entire process. To avoid such mistakes and missteps, we first must know how to recognize and anticipate them. The following questions ask you to think through what could go wrong. Note that answering these questions requires vulnerability. If it is any comfort to readers, the first author (Fulcher) has personally made fundamental missteps in every step of the improvement process and, even worse, did not recognize the mistakes at the time.

1. Provide examples from your own experiences where you have witnessed mistakes (or successes) in the following areas of learning improvement:
   a. building a collective will to improve
   b. carefully specifying what the learning is that should be improved
   c. collecting baseline information about the learning environment and/or students' abilities
   d. developing or adopting interventions
   e. implementing the interventions
   f. reassessing the learning environment and/or students' abilities
2. Reflect on the experiences you described. For the mistakes, why were they detrimental to achieving learning improvement at scale? For the successes, why were they useful?
3. If you were part of a learning improvement at-scale team, what processes would you have difficulty contributing to? Who within your program or institution has strengths that could compensate for your gaps? (Recall that learning improvement at scale is a team endeavor. It works when the collective brings out its individual members' strengths and compensates for individual members' weaknesses.)

PART TWO

A STEP-BY-STEP GUIDE TO IMPROVING LEARNING AT SCALE

4

TESTING THE COLLECTIVE
WILL TO IMPROVE

Before a learning improvement project can be launched at scale, a critical mass of faculty must commit to the process. This chapter provides advice regarding how to garner this commitment. We will discuss the importance of approaching improvement with the right mindset, choosing an area for the improvement project to target, and building a coalition among the people who will be involved in the project.

Learning improvement initiatives, almost invariably, cannot be carried on the back of a single faculty member. Spurring large-scale change initiatives requires garnering the support and commitment of colleagues and supervisors. But how do you know whether a program or department is ready to begin the process of improving student learning? This chapter will outline steps that learning improvement champions to be can take to gauge the interest, readiness, and commitment of their colleagues in the initial stages of an improvement initiative.

Xela modeled the attitudes and behaviors needed to launch learning improvement at scale. Fundamentally, Xela clearly cared about students and her colleagues. Specific to learning improvement, she realized that the inappropriate email handle incident reflected bigger concerns in her program, and she decided to do something about it. In other words, she had the right mindset for improvement: She believed that improvement was possible and that her actions could make a positive difference. Upon reflection, she realized that students struggled with aligning their writing to their audience. She knew this problem could be a "kiss of death" for a job or graduate school application, which points to her skill in choosing an appropriate skill to improve. Xela then identified colleagues who would be key to the project's success. She started with a trusted colleague before bringing the issue to the department head. With the department head's blessing, she strategically folded a broader group of allies into the effort. As a result of this well-planned process, Xela picked up a critical mass of faculty allies—a well-positioned coalition—who were ready and willing to join the improvement effort. Let's take a deeper dive into each of these areas, starting with mindset, to illuminate the rationale for this strategy.

The Precondition: A Learning Improvement Mindset

Many faculty members already exhibit the type of mindset and attitudes needed for learning improvement. Perhaps most importantly, they prioritize student learning. They realize that the experiences they provide as educators have a huge impact on what students learn during college. They spend time thinking about students, learning environments, and the interaction between the two. Never content with the bare minimum, they are often thinking about (and testing out) new approaches in the pursuit of more effective learning experiences. They also realize that learning does not stop with their own courses. The learning experiences prior to and following their courses matter to students, particularly in disciplines where course content and skills build systematically on each other as the student progresses through the program of study (i.e., scaffolded learning). For example, if a math faculty member teaches introductory calculus, students need to enter the course with proficient algebra skills. Likewise, introductory calculus skills are prerequisites to the more advanced math courses students will take later in their programs. The calculus sections that one faculty member teaches in isolation, alone, will not be effective for students. The course is only relevant to the extent it links the courses before it to the courses after it (or to the experiences students will have in jobs or graduate school after they complete their major course of study). The point: Courses across a program should complement and build on each other so students can achieve high-level learning outcomes.

Not all faculty have such a mindset. Some see themselves as victims of circumstance (students who just won't come to office hours, a department that refuses to provide adequate resources, the overwhelming research expectations in a publish-or-perish academic system). They have an external locus of control and blame students, high school teachers, other faculty, and administrators for students' poor learning. Whether or not these frustrations are founded, adopting a defeatist attitude is not an effective first step in bringing about better student learning.

Of course, even the most proactive faculty members occasionally gripe about situational factors beyond their control. And, sometimes even the most curmudgeonly faculty members will openly reflect on their teaching. Nevertheless, those who prioritize learning and collaboration are best positioned for learning improvement initiatives. Preparation is enhanced further when the institution also prioritizes learning and learning improvement. (See chapter 10 for strategies that institutions can adopt to foster learning improvement.)

Choosing an Area to Improve

What should we try to improve? This is a question we often hear, although the true root of the question varies. For instance, one faculty member may struggle to identify anything that needs improvement. He might say, "Our assessment results suggest students are doing fine. We don't see any glaring problems. What is there to improve?" On the other extreme, some faculty are overwhelmed by the possibilities. "I would love to see my students' skills improve in a dozen areas," they might say. "How do we decide where to begin?"

Our philosophy is that almost any student skill can be improved. We may choose a skill so lacking that, at current levels, it prevents students from being successful in their future endeavors (advanced coursework, employment, or graduate school, for example). Alternatively, a relative strength could be a target for improvement. Even professionals hone their best skills. Think about painters trying to improve their brush technique, social scientists developing more clever and elegant experimental designs, or computer scientists trying to write more efficient code. Likewise, the faculty members in a program may choose to double down on an area that is already a relative strength in order to further differentiate the program's assets.

The fact that any skill could be improved on should not be taken to mean that all learning areas should be targeted simultaneously. Attempting to improve everything at once typically results in nothing being improved at all. For example, we worked with one university that aimed to improve students' writing, critical thinking, and information literacy skills in one 1st-year seminar. Why stop there? As long they were riding a wave of delusion, why not throw in hieroglyphic translation and watch repair?

As a practical matter, we advocate for targeting a single clearly defined student learning area at a time for improvement. Excessively broad areas—like critical thinking, writing, or information literacy—may present challenges because they likely require improvement on a variety of subskills in order to demonstrate improvement in the overall area.

For example, consider the enormity of writing nonfiction essays, science fiction books, emails, text messages, memos, website content. Each requires its own approach to organization, style, mechanics, and audience awareness. No wonder Xela's group chose a subskill within writing as their targeted learning area. Absent tremendous resources and a lengthy timeline, attempting to improve multiple broad areas simultaneously (e.g., writing, critical thinking, and information literacy) will likely be frustratingly difficult and, ultimately, fruitless.

We suspect that our readers picked up this book with an idea of a construct (a defined, specific area of knowledge, a skill, or an ability) to improve already in mind. But what if that was not the case? How does one go about selecting an area to improve? We introduce three practical approaches for selecting a focal construct: the deductive approach, the inductive approach, and following an external mandate. We then provide guidance regarding what situations might favor which approach.

Deductive Approach

The deductive approach reflects the traditional, assessment-centered approach to improvement. A learning area is targeted for improvement because assessment data indicate that students are not performing as expected. Faculty look at the area most in need (i.e., the area where results are most disappointing), and then act on that area.

We observed one midsize university effectively use this approach. Senior psychology students took the ETS major field exam, which measures students' knowledge in six field domains: memory and cognition; perception, sensation, and physiology; developmental psychology; clinical and abnormal psychology; social psychology; and measurement and methodology. The program received feedback on students' performance in each area as well as comparisons to other schools across the nation. In five of the six areas, students scored above the 75th percentile. The faculty were pleased with this performance. However, students' developmental psychology scores sat around the 50th percentile, considerably lower than the other areas. Furthermore, 3 years of data confirmed the result wasn't a fluke; it was a trend. The faculty decided to focus their efforts on developmental psychology as a learning improvement area.

Inductive Approach

This approach veers outside of the information illuminated by assessment findings. Here, potential areas for improvement are identified through the experiences of the faculty (or the students). Conversations among colleagues and discussions about students' experiences during or after the program are two ways to spark ideas. In Xela's case, faculty members illuminated an area of learning that fell outside of the existing program structure and assessment apparatus. When they considered the problem carefully, it was clear that the existing SLOs and curriculum did not address an important learning area. In their case, the concept wasn't completely new: the psychology program already assessed some forms of writing. However, the program did not have an outcome related to students' ability to tailor their writing to a given situation, audience, and context. Because this was not an outcome for the program, their assessment data could not be used to gauge students' current performance in the area. Thus writing, as a construct, was underrepresented.

External Mandates

Most programs are, to varying degrees, beholden to powers beyond their own faculty. At the more extreme end, disciplinary accreditation often requires tightly regulated standards, curriculum, and testing. In these cases, a disciplinary call for improvement in a particular domain may be mandated by the accrediting body or professional organization. On the less extreme end, upper administrators might encourage academic programs to collaborate on a university-wide effort. For example, our own institution began an effort to enhance student research. In support of that effort, James Madison University's (JMU) assessment and faculty development offices released a request for proposals to elicit learning improvement projects intended to improve students' research skills.

Which Selection Approach Is Best?

In years past, we might have advocated for the deductive approach (the traditional assessment approach to improvement) over the inductive or external mandate approaches. Our implicit logic was that faculty should not move forward with decision-making, such as choosing an area to improve, until being informed by high-quality local data. To be in such a position, a program must already have a robust assessment process based on trustworthy measures, a data collection design that represents students accurately, and analyses that appropriately identify differences in performance across subskills and/or across various cohorts. In the pursuit of the deductive approach, we have observed many programs, year after year, trying to improve their assessment so they can eventually make decisions to improve learning. All too often, unfortunately, the yearly tweaks to the assessment process never evolve into changes to the underlying program.

The assessment process takes center stage, and the goal of improving student learning is sidelined.

If Maria used a deductive mindset when Rusty and Xela came to her, she might have requested that they hold off on the improvement talk. She might require that they first set up a good assessment process to measure contextually aligned writing. Only with data in hand would they be able to begin determining whether an improvement initiative is warranted.

The problem is that it would take at least 2 years before the program had quality data to even decide if writing should be improved. Continuing with this alternative reality, Xela and Rusty would have to convince their colleagues to spend an incredible amount of time and energy on assessing writing well to perhaps make changes in a few years. This is unlikely to be a compelling argument to time-strapped colleagues.

The approach taken by Xela, Rusty, and Maria (an inductive approach) was much more effective given their context. With support from their colleagues they had already decided that writing needed to improve absent quality assessment data. They spent their energy on determining *how* they should improve, not *if* they should improve.

They made bold, targeted changes to their program *and* developed a robust assessment process to determine the ways in which students improved and by how much. They waited on baseline information before intervening, but the decision to intervene was made before baseline data were collected. Stated another way, the deductive approach requires existing high-quality baseline learning data on a program first, then deciding if the program should improve, and then intervening. An inductive approach involves deciding to improve first, then collecting baseline data, then intervening.

We still advocate for strong assessment, of course, especially in the service of learning improvement. Finding or developing strong assessment tools and using them to collect data about the program is an essential early step in the learning improvement process. Nevertheless, we do not believe that a strong internal assessment process must be present on a student learning outcome before deciding to embark on an improvement project.

Our goal now is to see more evidence of learning improvement in higher education, regardless of how the process is initiated. Accordingly, we encourage faculty—alone, in small groups, or in tandem with the entire program faculty—to select areas to improve using the approach that works best for them. Programs with strong disciplinary accrediting bodies may be more inclined to action via external mandates. Strong preexisting program-level assessment systems, and the data they provide, may lead other programs to embrace the deductive approach. Any program struck by a faculty member's "aha!" moment may be moved by the inductive approach. Openness to the inductive approach also allows faculty to examine their program for blind spots: content or skills that are not being taught or assessed that, perhaps, should be. No matter the approach, the targeted learning area must be important to students' long-term success, and it must entice a critical mass of faculty.

Building the Learning Improvement Coalition

In the learning improvement projects in which we have participated, one faculty member typically identifies an improvement area initially. Recall, however, that for most programs, learning improvement requires cooperation and coordination among many faculty members in order to affect all students in the program. This section describes how to transition from one or two improvement-inclined faculty into a collective movement. The first step is to identify areas in the program where the learning environment might be changed. The second step is to gain the support of the faculty who work in that area. Here, we ask the following questions: Where in the program should changes be made? How can the faculty who teach those courses be convinced to partner in the process?

Locating Opportunities for Change in the Learning Environment

The intention of learning improvement at scale is to improve the learning of *all* students at the program level or higher. For example, if a learning improvement initiative is launched in the physics program, the intention is that all physics students will be impacted by the alterations to the learning environment by the time they graduate. If we want to make targeted changes to the learning environment, we must first identify parts of the physics program that allow faculty to affect all students.

Consider how most academic programs are structured. Students take some combination of compulsory and elective courses to fulfill a program of study. The exact number of courses and the mix of compulsory and elective courses varies considerably from program to program. Because the goal is to affect all students in the program, the clearest path to do so is through compulsory courses (or other compulsory program components). How those courses are staffed varies considerably and is largely influenced by the size of the program. In very small programs (e.g., a minor or a certificate program), a single faculty member may be responsible for teaching all courses. In this type of program, a successful improvement project could be launched using solely that one willing faculty member.

Larger programs might provide multiple sections of a given course. For example, approximately 150 sections of JMU's general education writing course are taught annually by over 40 instructors. Some instructors are tenured or tenure-track faculty members, and others are adjuncts or non-tenure-track instructors. A small number of instructors are graduate students. If this course were to be targeted for a learning improvement project, each of those 40 instructors would have to buy into the process, as well as the department head who oversees this area.

Some programs are even trickier. One of our general education areas—arts and humanities—requires all students to complete three courses among 10 offered. The total number of sections and instructors is similar to that of the general education writing course mentioned earlier. The difference, however, is that the 40-plus faculty are spread out across several departments and the 10 course options. Therefore, to get all these faculty in sync, multiple department heads would also need to be in sync. Possible, of course, but more challenging.

No simple, standardized approach can be offered to guide the process of identifying willing, invested colleagues to embark on a learning improvement project. The following four steps, flexibly applied, can serve as guidelines:

1. Identify all the compulsory courses that could be a theoretical fit for the improvement initiative. This serves two purposes. First, it forces careful thought about the program's coverage of the learning area. Second, it quickly narrows down the scope of courses to be considered.
2. For each of the courses identified in the first step, list all instructors. This list provides you with the people who may be involved in the eventual intervention chain.
3. Identify potential allies like the department head, dean, assessment professionals, and faculty developers. Those identified will provide you with a sense of your potential support network.
4. Using the lists created in the first three steps, create a visual representation of the courses, the instructors, and other allies. Use this visual to plan your approach.
   a. Who would likely be the champion(s)?
   b. Which people are connected to each other?
   c. Who will likely be interested in collaborating?
   d. Who should be approached about the project, and in what order?

Let's examine how this process might look in two different programs: one that is relatively simple structurally, and another that is somewhat more complex. Table 4.1 contrasts a certificate program in automotive mechanics (where two faculty cover all the required courses) with Xela's program (where a much larger number of faculty members are responsible for teaching the required courses).

In Program 1, Bill and Ted are the only instructors of the five required courses. If they wanted to collaborate, they could plan changes that would affect students in each of the five courses. However, even if only one of them was on board, he would have the capacity to make program-level differences himself. For example, Bill might decide to make changes in 175 and 201. Given that he is the sole faculty member teaching these courses, and all students are required to take both, he could single-handedly make program-level modifications to the learning environment.

Of course, many programs are bigger than Program 1. In larger programs (e.g., Program 2, representing Xela and Rusty's department), program-level changes are more complicated. They can require the collaboration and coordination of many faculty members. The table displays the seven required courses in the psychology program. Even if we only consider the courses which all students are required to complete, it is clear that any improvement effort would require a good deal of coordination. If Xela's program wished to

TABLE 4.1
Instructors Teaching Required Courses in Two Programs

Course*	Instructor(s)
Program 1	
175	Bill
201	Bill
242	Ted
261	Bill and Ted
282	Bill and Ted
Program 2	
180	Jason, Crystal, Ali, Sasha, Theresa
201	Jessica, Xela, Gabe, Yelisey, Rebecca
275	Miguel, Kevin, Sasha
290	Clarice, Jen, Jorge, Omar
310	Kurt, Shaun, Kevin, Ali, Gus
362	Shaun, Andrea, Theresa
495	Katherine, Rusty, Andrea, Daigo, Theresa

*Elective courses not displayed

change the learning environment by altering even a single course listed in the table, at least three unique instructors would need to collaborate.

How to Bring Faculty on Board

In small programs like the automotive mechanics example just provided, there is no need for coalition building because a single faculty member can influence all students through a required course. At this stage in the learning improvement process, individuals in such cases only have to convince themselves to take action. However, small programs are often housed in small institutions. They may not have access to full-time assessment experts or professional developers. They either must build up expertise internally (e.g., Ted earns an online assessment certificate) or rely on external consultants for assistance.

In larger programs, like Xela's, the efforts of a single faculty member are unlikely to be sufficient. Fortunately, there are several ways to bring faculty on board. The first we will call the "individual to the masses," which was the approach Xela took. In this approach, a single person acts as the hub for the initiative. Other people are folded into the process as it continues, but the initial action is taken by one person. Recall that Xela did the following:

- spotted the problem and determined that it was relevant to the rest of the psychology program;
- identified cochampion(s) with whom to discuss her ideas early on;
- discussed her plans with the department head early in the process;
- gauged the interest level of a critical mass of faculty;
- investigated support and resistance among her colleagues; and
- worked with the course leads to form a supportive "inner circle" prior to involving all program faculty in the improvement effort.

As Xela developed her ideas, she slowly expanded the number of people with whom she collaborated. By the time she brought the planned initiative to the rest of her department, she had already garnered the support of two key allies: Rusty (her cochampion) and Maria (her department head). Later, the inner circle acted as a sounding board for the initiative prior to the involvement of a larger group of faculty members.

Another approach is to "meet in the middle." This is similar to the approach previously outlined, but it is initiated by a midlevel administrator instead of a faculty member. In this approach, the administrator offers support for an improvement initiative but leaves the learning area to be decided by the program faculty. Imagine if Maria used her position as department head to initiate interest and action on improvement. She may do something like this:

- Indicate in a department meeting that she would like to support a learning improvement initiative within one of the department's programs. She explains the overall process at the outset. Wanting the project to be driven by faculty expertise and judgment, she solicits ideas from her colleagues using the example questions at the end of the chapter.
- Ask faculty members to present their ideas and advocate for their importance.
- Survey the faculty in the room to see the degree of support for each.
- Support the learning area that garners the most enthusiasm.

Finally, the last approach might be to "bring the top down to earth." As we discussed earlier, universities, professional organizations, and disciplinary accrediting bodies often disperse big initiatives from the top, hoping (or requiring) that individual programs will participate. The problem with orders from "on high" is that faculty tend to have high standards for determining whether they will invest their energy in a new initiative or project. They must be convinced that the initiative will be beneficial. Often, it is the department head or program director who attempts to get instructors on board with such initiatives.

Imagine Maria is asked whether her program might be interested in participating in the university's new ethical reasoning initiative. How might she approach this situation?

- First, Maria would need to get up to speed with the initiative. What is it about? What evidence is there that it is (or can be) successful? What support might the university offer to help her program get on board?
- Next, she would approach her program's faculty members openly in a meeting. She would need to explain how the initiative fits in with the department's programming, what the project would entail, and what support would be provided. Then, she would need to evaluate their openness to considering the proposal.
- If the department's faculty members are open to the project, Maria would need to bring in a representative from the ethical reasoning initiative. The representative needs to further convince faculty that the initiative aligns with their interests. This representative might start by asking about ethical situations in the field of psychology that students

may need to navigate after they graduate. How does the program equip alumni to approach those situations? What happens if alumni are unable to navigate ethical situations? Further, the representative needs to show that being part of the initiative provides faculty with resources and/or expertise that they would not have without it.

If there is a critical mass of faculty who agree to participate in the project, then the problem-solving process can begin.

Closing Thoughts

Except in very small programs, learning improvement is a team sport. It takes a group of collaborative faculty members who believe in, and will contribute to, a better learning environment for students. Key to launching a successful learning improvement initiative is the careful selection of a target construct. This chapter provided several considerations for choosing what, exactly, an initiative should aim to improve. As with all group efforts worth pursuing, careful attention to group dynamics, collaboration, and openness to feedback are critical components in learning improvement.

A Note About Exercises

At the end of each chapter in Part Two, we provide several exercises intended to increase your facility with the concepts covered therein. As in the previous section, the exercises can be completed by you alone, but may be more useful (and fun) if worked through by a small team.

We suggest first addressing the exercises as if they were practice. For example, pick a program with which you (and your colleagues, if you are working through this book together) are familiar and construct a hypothetical progression of a learning improvement process as suggested in the chapters in Part 2. In doing so, you will gain a holistic perspective of the most relevant considerations for learning improvement. Think of the exercises as being akin to hypothetical case studies.

When you begin a real-life learning improvement project, the steps will unfold more slowly. If you have completed the exercises in this book, you will be in a better position to predict how your decisions will impact later steps of the project. In other words, read the book and complete the exercises first before embarking on a learning improvement project. Then use the book as a resource as you initiate and implement a learning improvement project.

We hope you will use these exercises to plan for a learning improvement initiative and begin to develop your coalition.

Exercises

Recall that picking a student learning area and building an improvement coalition are early, necessary conditions for a successful learning improvement project.

1. Practice picking an area to improve using the three approaches discussed in chapter 4.
    a. Deductive approach: If your program submits an assessment report on student learning, obtain a copy of the report. Based on the information in the report, what area would you suggest your program work on?
    b. Inductive approach: What knowledge, skills, or attitudes do students need that are not currently emphasized in your program? Lean on your own experience and intuition, and don't be afraid to converse with your colleagues. When students graduate from your program, are they missing any skills that might help them get a job? Be successful in their next level of education? Better navigate life?
    c. External mandates: Do leaders or other authorities in your discipline suggest there should be a new skill added to the curriculum? A disciplinary journal or a major professional organization might be a place to start looking for this information. How might a focus group be conducted with employers of your programs' graduates? What questions would you ask? Is there a particular skill, set of knowledge, or disposition needed in the workplace that your students don't currently have?
    d. Out of all learning areas you selected through the various methods, which one resonates with you the most? Why? Make a brief argument for why your program should focus on this area.
2. Practice thinking through a learning improvement area. For this exercise, it's not critical that you pick the "right" area to improve. Just pick any construct you can imagine your program working on.
    a. Identify all the experiences and courses in your program that are compulsory for all students.
    b. Which of those courses/experiences might be logical places to make changes to the learning environment, in support of the learning area you identified?
    c. Of those courses/experiences you identified, visually represent each of the instructors in each of those areas (see Table 4.1 for an example). These are the instructors who would need to be on board for the

intervention. How will you get them involved? If you see multiple instructors for a given course who are unlikely to collaborate under any circumstances, then you might have to remove that course from the realm of possible courses.

d. Add to your illustration other people who are critical to or who could be helpful in your learning improvement quest. Think about the program's director and/or the department head. Consider adding in higher-level administrators, assessment professionals, faculty developers, and so on. Who might support your project?

e. Now that all the players are depicted visually, indicate how you will navigate this group. Will you first identify a cochampion or two, then go to the department head, and then to the masses, as Xela did? Or will you take another approach? What makes the most sense in your context?

5

VISION

This purpose of this chapter is to address a fundamental question: What exactly do we want students to know, think, or do after a successful learning improvement project? A clear and concrete vision of future students focuses the learning improvement process.

Vision is an essential component of leadership. It transports teams from loose ideas to concrete plans, providing sustenance when energy flags. Vision is also a powerful component of learning improvement. We begin by envisioning, in an ideal world, what our students would look like upon completion of our program. What do they know, think, or do *better* than graduates of the program as it currently stands? Why do these improvements matter to their lives? To their employers? To society? This chapter describes the important steps in the visioning of student learning improvement:

- developing a loose idea into a formal vision statement,
- refining the vision statement into SLOs, and
- concretizing SLOs through the creation of assessment specifications and items.

In chapter 2, we saw Xela and her colleagues' vision develop throughout each of these stages. First, Xela's frustrating experience with a student's email etiquette morphed into broader concerns about students' written communication abilities. After some thought and planning with her colleague Rusty, she was able to leverage her budding idea—*what if we could help our students communicate more effectively?*—to gain interest among her colleagues. The collective faculty then began asking what it would look like if students could effectively adjust their writing for different contexts. The faculty's thinking

71

began shifting from day-to-day tasks toward imagining how students would be better equipped for life after college if this skill was strengthened. Eventually, Xela and her colleagues drafted a formal vision statement, outlining what they hoped to achieve for the students graduating from their program. With the vision in hand, they wrote SLOs that specifically identified the components of communication (specifically, contextually appropriate writing) on which their efforts would focus. The ultimate articulation of the vision was the creation of an assessment instrument carefully crafted to measure the degree to which students could write effectively in different contexts. Table 5.1 shows the evolution of the team's process.

The ultimate goal of the visioning process goes beyond achieving a well-aligned set of SLOs and assessment tools. In addition, this step must also ensure that the other people involved in the program (particularly the people who will be implementing the intervention) buy into the process. In practice, we have seen visions intended to inspire teams but ultimately drive a single person. Such instances rarely, if ever, result in learning improvement at scale. In the following pages, we will use Xela and Rusty's story to demonstrate how to make visioning a community effort.

Involving Stakeholders: Who Does What (and When)?

The point of developing a strong vision is to guide a group of people to achieve a common goal. However, it is *not* the case that garnering support requires everyone to take part equally at every step in the process. On paper, it seems reasonable to maximize involvement: If we want everyone to be equally committed to the initiative, it makes sense that we would solicit equal amounts of feedback from all participants. In practice, though, this method can easily spiral out of control if more than a handful of people are involved in the vision development process. In Xela and Rusty's case, 15 people were part of the improvement process: two cochampions (Xela and Rusty), three faculty leads joining them in the "inner circle," and 10 additional faculty members in the outer circle. Imagine our cochampions trying to craft a vision statement and SLOs, from scratch, with more than a dozen people attempting to coauthor simultaneously. We've seen meetings like this where an hour is spent debating a single word. At that rate, a sentence might take a day, and a paragraph a week. Louder voices inevitably dominate, defeating the initial purpose of equal involvement. How, then, should the desire for input and buy-in be balanced with the time-bound pressures of improvement attempts?

To be clear, everyone involved *should* have input at multiple stages in the process. However, it is unlikely that involving everyone to the same

TABLE 5.1
Steps to Articulation of Vision

Stage	Purpose	Example From Xela's Department
Loose idea	Provides a launching point for conversations about student learning and possibilities for improvement.	Frustration over a student providing an inappropriate email address on a job application led to larger concerns about students' abilities to communicate appropriately in a variety of contexts.
Vision statement	Identifies why the learning area is important as well as a general framing of the construct.	"We envision graduating students who are capable of meeting the demands of writing in graduate school and professional life. Our students will be able to analyze an array of writing contexts and deftly implement appropriate strategies for effective writing."
SLOs	Provides the thesis statement of a student learning improvement project. Summarizes what the program wants students to know, think, or do relative to the targeted learning area.	Upon graduating from the psychology program, students will • recognize the elements of a writing context that influence appropriate choice of writing strategy; • explain the reasons for differences among written communication styles relevant to psychological research, scientific communication, and professional workplaces; and • demonstrate the ability to write about the same content for a number of different audiences, purposes, and occasions
Assessment specifications	Clearly defined parameters identifying behaviors or work products that indicate student proficiency in the targeted learning area.	The team developed three measures to assess student proficiency: • Multiple-choice measure designed to assess students' ability to identify relevant stylistic conventions and contextual considerations when approaching writing tasks • Performance assessment requiring students to evaluate and (if necessary) revise a brief text in order to meet the demands of a provided writing context • An embedded assessment designed to assess students' ability to write about the same content in different contexts

degree at all stages is an effective strategy. Instead, consider who will take primary responsibility for the effort, who will provide in-depth feedback, and who will review close-to-final products. In the case of Xela and Rusty, we can think of the team of implementers as consisting of three concentric circles with the cochampions in the center ring, the three course leaders (the "inner circle") in the middle ring, and the other 10 faculty members in the outer circle (see Figure 5.1). The cochampions are typically the drafters of documents and ideas. They are the primary drivers of progress, and they commit the most time to the project. The course leaders provide extensive feedback that shapes the approach. The additional members of the intervention chain in the outer circle provide intermittent feedback on more polished drafts. The cochampions' job is to ensure that these feedback loops are well integrated.

Importantly, all members of the implementation team (regardless of the ring in which they are placed) must be team players. They are selected for participation because of their willingness to collaborate and compromise. If the champions have devoted sufficient attention to the coalition-building process, the group is unlikely to contain saboteurs. Nevertheless, it is important to ensure that key members of the implementation team (and leaders in the department or institution) have some say in their placement. For example, it is prudent to ask the department head to choose their "ring" early in the process. At the very least, they should be included in the conversations to stay informed. Departmental politics and social dynamics will play an important role in the placement of people into rings, so this process should

Figure 5.1. Relationship between cochampions, inner circle, and outer circle.

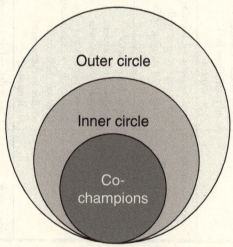

not be taken lightly. Regardless of final decisions, though, vision refinement must be intentionally coupled with decisions about who will provide different degrees of input at different times in the process.

Refining Ideas Into Vision Statements

Once the implementation team's organization has been established, the visioning process can begin in earnest. At this point, goals for the improvement effort are likely to be more concrete than when they were first derived, but not yet formalized into a vision statement. When asked what aspect of student learning is to be improved, the response usually covers a large learning territory: critical thinking, writing, professionalism, creativity. These broad areas are informed by one of the improvement selection strategies outlined in chapter 4 (i.e., deductive, inductive, or external mandates). Determining a general target area is an important first step. In order to facilitate strategic action, though, "writing" or some other learning mega-construct must be further deconstructed.

As an analogy, imagine a family wants to adopt a pet but never plans specific details. The less the family discusses their needs and constraints for their future pet, the less likely they are to follow through with a successful adoption. In contrast, imagine the family begins discussing their plans and desires in more depth. What kind of pet do they want? How much time and energy will they be able to devote to its care? What kind of animal do they have space for in their home? Do any of them have allergies? What about phobias? These questions would flesh out a vision for their future pet that will eventually influence action. Aiming for a low-maintenance addition to the family will result in a very different decision than seeking out a four-legged running buddy. If the family knows, for example, that they desire an energetic companion and that they have a securely fenced yard, they can begin looking for an animal (e.g., a medium- or large-sized dog of an active breed) that fit these criteria.

Similarly, we need to clarify intentions for the learning improvement initiative early in the process so that outcomes, interventions, and measures can be planned and evaluated for appropriateness. One of our favorite approaches is to gather a group of faculty members in a program and dive into their thoughts on a construct. The first author affectionately refers to these meetings as "riffing sessions." The general construct is determined prior to the meeting, but the riffing session serves to explicate the components of the construct, its importance to students and other stakeholders, and the appearance of high- and low-quality manifestations of the construct. For example, consider a group of faculty members committed to improving students' writing skills. We might ask the following questions:

- What does good writing look like in your program?
- Can you tell me about a student you've taught who had excellent writing skills? What did they do (or not do) that was so exceptional?
- What does poor student writing look like in your program?
- Can you tell me about a student who had particularly poor writing skills? What did they do (or not do) that was so problematic?
- What does it look like to write professionally in your field?
- What components of writing are especially important to your students' success?
- How might better writing skills benefit students while they are still in your program?
- How might better writing skills benefit students after graduation?
- Does your field have a robust scholarship of teaching and learning literature base? If so, does it contain guidance about teaching writing in your field? What are the current best practices outlined in the literature?

A scribe writes down the responses, allowing participants to engage freely in conversation. As a group, we then look for themes. The point of the exercise is for faculty to explore their schemas of a learning territory and, perhaps, prioritize different aspects of the territory. Ideally, after the session is complete, the participants (including any participating assessment professionals or faculty developers) can clearly identify specific elements of the larger construct on which to focus.

We want to draw attention to the final bullet, which references the field's scholarship of teaching and learning. This question is designed to gauge whether the group has researched the topic before the meeting. If this research has not yet been conducted, the initiative is not doomed. However, it does highlight a crucial next step. Many general constructs (e.g., writing) have been defined, debated, and researched by armies of scholars long before a department embarks on a learning improvement journey. Before going too far down the path of refining a loose idea on their own, we strongly encourage educators to examine existing literature. Recall that Xela and Rusty began reading articles about writing early in the process and found that several researchers had explored similar topics (both within their discipline and in metacognition research). Xela and Rusty referred to this body of literature at various points in their learning improvement process. The importance of early and frequent consultation with the literature cannot be overstated.

A useful starting point for literature reviews is Educational Testing Services' (ETS, n.d.) foundational framework papers that were developed in support of the ETS HEIghten tests. These documents summarize various theoretical conceptualizations of important learning outcomes, existing research, and available tests in a variety of areas relevant to higher education. These reports can provide a survey of common constructs while providing avenues for additional research. We acknowledge that these framework papers are associated with ETS' own tests. Regardless, we have often found them to be useful in the early stages of understanding a construct.

No matter where the literature review begins, there are two basic questions that the process (and ensuing faculty conversations) must answer. The first is why the chosen area is so important for student success. Being able to provide a good answer is critical for eventually gathering support for the initiative. A learning improvement initiative cannot occur unless this argument can be made effectively. The second question is a more specific version of the first: Which facets of the construct will be the focus of the initiative? This level of specificity is necessary for writing a good vision statement (and, down the line, creating strong outcomes and measures).

Xela and her colleagues addressed both questions in their work to improve students' context-specific writing skills. Recall that Xela began her process by writing down all the examples she could think of that displayed issues with students' ability to appropriately tailor their communication to the demands of a given situation. From there, she narrowed her attention to students' context-specific writing skills. Partnering with Rusty, the budding team began to examine the existing literature on writing in undergraduate psychology programs and developing students' metacognition. They made the case to their colleagues that improving students' skills in these areas would likely have important repercussions on employability and graduate school admission rates. They consulted with their learning improvement coaches and faculty leads to draft a vision statement, which was eventually agreed on by all 15 people in the intervention chain:

> We envision graduating students who are capable of meeting the demands of writing in graduate school and professional life. Our students will be able to analyze an array of writing contexts and deftly implement appropriate strategies for effective writing.

Note how their vision statement captures why the target skill is important ("demands of writing in graduate school and professional life") and begins to clarify aspects of the construct ("our students will be able to analyze an array of writing contexts and deftly implement appropriate strategies for effective writing"). These are the building blocks for SLOs.

From Vision Statement to SLOs

Articulating a vision for student learning is an iterative process, and drafting SLOs is a critical step in advancing the vision. A vision statement is akin to a 30-second commercial for learning improvement, while an SLO is more like a thesis statement. In order to draft the outcomes, faculty involved in the improvement initiative must consider what a student meeting the vision should know, think, or do upon graduation. SLOs are operationalized versions of the vision, providing examples of the kinds of actions or work products that would demonstrate achievement of the vision. Thus, they tend to be more fine-grained than the vision statement. For example, consider the outcomes drafted by Xela, Rusty, and their colleagues:

Upon graduating from the psychology program, students will

- recognize the elements of a writing context that influence appropriate choice of writing strategy;
- explain the reasons for differences among written communication styles relevant to psychological research, scientific communication, and professional workplaces; and
- demonstrate the ability to write about the same content for a number of different audiences, purposes, and occasions.

These outcomes build on the vision statement by specifying the specific elements of writing to be targeted by the learning improvement project. The first SLO identifies a basic skill that acts as a building block for effective context-specific writing: Can students identify the contextual elements that dictate effective writing approaches? The second SLO identifies the theoretical considerations of writing choices. The final SLO concerns students' ability to demonstrate their skills by writing about a common topic in a variety of contexts. Each of these outcomes flows clearly from the vision while providing additional detail and specificity. Examination of the outcomes tells an interested audience what a student should know, think, or do upon graduating from the program.

From SLOs to Assessment Specifications and Items

Earlier in this chapter, we made a bold statement that assessment instruments can be the ultimate articulation of vision. Here, we will reflect on that statement, as it might come as a surprise. In our experience, some faculty consider tests a necessary evil, an appendage of the learning process. At best, they are considered a weak reflection of desired learning. For those educators, the phrase "teaching to the test" has a negative connotation, referring to a watered-down curriculum intended to match a necessarily limited measure.

We like to think about assessment differently. Problems occur when the links among learning vision, SLOs, the learning environment, and testing tools become uncoupled (Prendergast & Fulcher, 2019). The test often shoulders the blame, but in reality, a "bad test" is often symptomatic of a broken learning system. Some tests are certainly flawed; it would be dishonest of us to claim otherwise. However, it is often easier to blame a test for bad student performance than to admit there is a problem with the program's treatment of certain SLOs.

We argue that a thoughtful test selection or development process forces faculty to think deeply about student learning. What types of student behaviors would reflect attainment of the vision? Assessment experts and faculty developers typically advocate for selecting or creating a test before developing a curriculum. This approach is often called backward design (Wiggins & McTighe, 2005). In other words, figure out what behaviors you would like students to be able to perform at the end of a learning experience, articulate the behaviors through the development or identification of an assessment tool, and then reverse engineer the learning environment so that students develop the skills (Crocker, 2003; Fink, 2013). If the assessment tasks or questions are an accurate reflection of what we want students to learn, then "teaching to the test" takes on a new meaning. The test items, in essence, operationalize the vision. Teaching with test achievement in mind, then, means teaching with the goal of achieving the vision.

Test Selection or Test Development?

Of course, in order to align a measure to outcomes and curriculum, we must obtain or create some sort of a measure. Measurement tools can take many forms, including performance assessments, portfolios, attitudinal scales, and multiple-choice tests. (Throughout this book, we use the words *measures* and *assessment tools* to refer to the broad spectrum of options for assessing students' knowledge, skills, attitudes, and abilities.) The decision to use an existing measure or create a new one is an important one.

In many situations, test selection is the most viable option. First, quality tests have been constructed for several constructs. Why reinvent the wheel? Additionally, many available tests have been created by teams of content experts, test developers, and psychometricians. Technical expertise in each of these areas is extremely important for the development of high-quality measurement tools. In contrast, most university programs do not have access to these resources or expertise. Even though most of these tests come with a price tag, the expense is almost always less than creating a high-quality test locally.

Before dispensing guidance on how to select a test, let us first illustrate how a "good" test may be part of a bad assessment process. Imagine a midlevel administrator unilaterally deciding to buy a test after being persuaded by a salesperson at a professional conference. The salesperson paints a picture of an accreditation crackdown in higher education and offers a quick solution: purchasing the test. How might this scenario play out? Not well. The administrator may cobble together a convenience sample of students in nonoptimal conditions to take the test. Most faculty members remain unaware that testing is taking place. When the test results come back, the administrator shares them with the faculty members, who proceed to poke holes in the data collection ("That sample wasn't representative"). They poke holes in the contents of the test ("This test doesn't even measure what we think is important"). And, most damning, they poke holes in the communication ("We didn't know this was going on"). These conditions, needless to say, are not conducive to effective use of assessment results.

We suggest a different approach when solidifying measures for an improvement effort. First, we suggest that the core team begins the process by searching for existing tests online. They may find some options are available that match their needs. Companies often provide helpful information about their tests (cost, intended uses, assessment specifications, and administration details) online. The team can then compare this information against their targeted SLOs, seeking to find the measure (or measures) that best fit their needs. The group then has the opportunity to select the most promising three or four tests and request confidential review copies from the publishers. Most companies will agree to provide sample materials in return for a written agreement of nondisclosure.

The core team may then examine each test, item by item, to determine which items align with the targeted SLOs. The goal is to determine which items are good indicators of the learning vision. This specific process is called a backward translation (Sundre & Thelk, 2010) and is part of what many testing experts would refer to as "content validation" (see American Educational Research Association et al. (2014) for a far more extensive discussion of validity evidence based on test content). If a high percentage of a test's items cover your program's targeted SLOs, then the test can be retained as a candidate for adoption. Importantly, members of all rings of the implementation team can provide feedback in this process. For example, the champions may take primary responsibility for identifying measures, obtaining review copies, and conducting the backward translation. Their preliminary decisions then may be handed off and reviewed by the inner circle whose feedback is critical to making a final decision in tandem with the outer circle. While it is unlikely that a test will provide a perfect match to the SLOs, the goal is to achieve agreement from all members of the intervention chain that the measure is reasonable. This prevents the (unfortunately quite common) situation in which results are dismissed upon receipt because of disagreements about the measure's merits.

The first author (Fulcher) worked with a university's general education committee on just such a process. The committee had articulated clear SLOs for scientific reasoning but did not yet have an assessment instrument. Because they had neither the time nor the resources to create a high-quality test from scratch, they opted to select an existing multiple-choice test. A subcommittee evaluated three proprietary tests against the general scientific reasoning SLOs using a backward design process. One test came out the clear winner, and the institution used that test in their practice. Not only did it match up well to the SLOs, the faculty subcommittee was well acquainted with the quality of the alignment, which helped downstream when results were defended to other faculty members.

In some cases, institutions start with an existing instrument and modify it to better match their SLOs. Many prominent examples of such practice include the Association of American Colleges & Universities' (AAC&U's) VALUE rubrics (Rhodes, 2010). For example, Filer and Steehler (2018) share a story from Roanoke College. Several instructors were hoping to design and pilot a rubric to evaluate writing in their courses. They soon realized they had limited experience with developing rubrics. As opposed to reinventing the wheel, they began with an existing instrument: AAC&U's Written Communication VALUE rubric. They then modified the instrument to better align with their needs.

Sometimes it can be challenging to find an existing test that conceptually maps with a program's SLOs. In general, the more atypical an SLO (or SLOs that focus on a narrower learning area), the lower the probability of finding a high-quality ready-made test. For example, our own institution began a project several years ago to improve students' ethical reasoning skills. Our conceptualization of ethical reasoning had been newly developed and was specific to our campus, so no existing instrument provided an adequate match. The situation therefore necessitated the creation of a new instrument (Sanchez et al., 2017). The process was arduous but worth it. The resulting assessment measure was exceptionally aligned with intended learning outcomes, the type of measure faculty would want to teach to. In fact, we have offered professional development for faculty who wish to teach ethical reasoning by having them evaluate ethical reasoning essays using the rubric.

After the workshop, many faculty members commented how understanding the rubric gave them a much better sense regarding what students should learn and what they should emphasize to help students develop ethical reasoning skills. Regarding further guidance for those readers interested in measurement principles, Bandalos (2018) serves as a detailed introduction to measurement theory. Schmeiser and Welch (2006) provide a good overview of test development. Haladyna et al. (2002) provide excellent suggestions for developing multiple-choice items, and Stiggins (1987) provides a helpful introduction to performance assessments tools (e.g., rubrics).

Xela and Rusty found themselves without a clear choice for their assessment strategy. While they found plenty of assessment tools that focused on writing, none focused on the nuances of writing about psychological concepts for a variety of contexts. Because they had an experienced assessment professional on their team as well as a writing expert, they decided to create their own instruments. The benefit of creating tests from scratch is that the tests can be customized to closely fit local SLOs. The drawback, of course, is that high-quality test development requires a great deal of work, time, data collection, and technical expertise. Depending on the construct and the stakes of the measurement, this process can take months or even years.

While backward design and test adaptation processes are helpful in obtaining a well-matched measure, they are far from the only necessary considerations when planning an assessment strategy. There are other reliability and validity issues to consider as well, which are best evaluated by someone with assessment and measurement expertise. While the psychometric dimensions of test evaluation are beyond the scope of this book, several excellent references on these topics are available (e.g., AERA et al., 2014; Lissitz, 2009).

Closing Thoughts

If done well, the visioning process can do two things for a burgeoning learning improvement project. First, it can provide clarity regarding what students might be able to do in the future. Second, it can be a vehicle for deepening the commitment of the learning improvement team. However, these outcomes of the visioning process are not to be taken for granted. Careful attention to who is consulted throughout the process (and to what degree they are consulted) is a necessary part of learning improvement leadership. Failure to adequately involve relevant faculty partners will likely result in a lack of buy-in from key participants; overinvolvement will likely slow down the speed of progress substantially. But if artfully managed, the visioning process represents a key step in creating a cohesive team and developing concrete goals for the learning improvement project.

Exercises

Practice refining a learning area.

1. Choose a general area of learning (the loose idea) that you think is important, perhaps the same one you chose in the chapter 4 exercises. Then, answer the following questions.
    a. What does good [insert your topic/skill here] look like in your program?
    b. Can you tell me about a student you've taught who had excellent [insert your topic/skill here]? What did they do (or not do) that was so exceptional?
    c. What does it look like to [insert your topic/skill here] professionally in your field?
    d. What does poor student [insert your topic/skill here] look like in your program?
    e. Can you tell me about a student who had particularly poor [insert your topic/skill here] skills? What did they do (or not do) that was so problematic?
    f. What components of [insert your topic/skill here] are especially important to your students' success?
    g. How might improved [insert your topic/skill here] skills benefit students after graduation?
    h. How might improved [insert your topic/skill here] skills benefit students while they are still in your program?
2. Investigate relevant scholarship of teaching and learning.
    a. Identify reputable literature in your field or adjacent fields (e.g., journals, books) that emphasize teaching and learning.
    b. List them and make a case for why you think they are reputable/why your colleagues should find them trustworthy.
    c. What do these resources say regarding the best practice of [insert your topic/skill here] in your field?
3. Develop the loose idea into a vision statement, then to SLOs, and finally into assessment specifications. Fill in Table 5.2 with your work. Note: This exercise can be completed in a couple of hours to get the gist. It can take several weeks or months if used in a real learning improvement project as the literature should be heavily integrated and collaboration should be maximized.

TABLE 5.2
Articulation of Vision: Your Example

Stage	Purpose	Your Example
Loose idea	Provides a launching point for conversations about student learning and possibilities for improvement.	
Vision statement	Identifies why the learning area is important as well as a general framing of the construct.	
SLOs	Provides the thesis statement of a student learning improvement project. Summarizes what the program wants students to know, think, or do relative to the targeted learning area.	
Assessment specifications	Clearly defined parameters identifying behaviors or work products that indicate student proficiency in the targeted learning area.	

6

WHERE ARE WE NOW?

*Determining the effectiveness of a new educational intervention is
futile without formal evaluation of baseline conditions in the program.
To understand how the program is operating, we need to measure how
students are performing and examine the program's current structure.
This chapter will outline the necessary steps in measuring baseline
student performance as well as gathering information about the
baseline educational conditions in the program.*

We have now arrived at the first step in the simple model for learning improvement: evaluating the baseline. A detailed understanding of the baseline program is necessary for guiding the learning improvement initiative and evaluating progress as the initiative proceeds. Once an area poised for improvement has been identified, pausing to evaluate the current context can be difficult. Energized about the possibility for a better learning environment (and better student learning), stakeholders will likely be tempted to push forward, making changes to their courses and cocurricular opportunities to make immediate strides toward elevating students' knowledge and skills.

In this chapter, we call for a slower approach. Ideally, by this point in the process, a great deal of time has been spent gathering information from key stakeholders within (and affiliated with) the program. Champions and an inner circle have been identified, and their relationships with the larger community have been leveraged to identify the needs and concerns of their colleagues. This process has hopefully resulted in sufficient support to move forward with the improvement initiative. This social element—the time and attention devoted to addressing concerns, the careful evaluation of roles, and consideration of the program's relationship to power structures both within and outside the university—lays crucial groundwork for the rest of the learning improvement project. Cutting corners on the remaining steps, as tempting as quick action may be, risks undoing the goodwill established earlier.

A careful, deliberate approach to evaluating the baseline requires attention to two very different elements of the program: student performance and the learning environment producing that performance. The former tends to receive the most attention. Most of us who work in higher education have an affinity for data, rooted in a deep desire to understand what students can do. Of course, obtaining baseline data about student performance is necessary for engaging in—and evidencing—learning improvement. However, this information must be supplemented with an evaluation of the baseline learning environment in order to be useful.

To demonstrate, we'll take a quick nostalgic detour. Some readers may recall advertisements for bodybuilding guides that were printed on the backs of old comic books. One particularly memorable example depicted a muscular bully kicking sand into the face of a slender protagonist (Charles Atlas Ltd., 1952). In the frames that follow, the man decides to exact revenge by purchasing a bodybuilding book. He eventually returns triumphant to the beach, confronts his bully, and strolls away as female onlookers swoon.

While this advertisement does an excellent job of depicting the baseline and post-intervention performance levels (in the form of the protagonist's physique), the baseline environmental conditions are ignored. In the case of the advertisement, we do not know what context and behaviors have contributed to the protagonist's physique: What was his exercise regimen? His diet? His overall health status? Imagine three different contexts from which his baseline physique may stem:

1. He consumes 1,000 calories daily, lifts weights five times per week, and is free from illness.
2. He consumes 2,500 calories daily, never lifts weights, and is free from illness.
3. He consumes 4,000 calories daily, lifts weights five times per week, and has a tapeworm.

These three baseline contexts, of course, require very different interventions if the goal is to gain muscle mass. For the first scenario, we would recommend additional caloric intake. For the second, the addition of a weightlifting regimen would be appropriate. In the final example, the extraction of the tapeworm is the primary concern. But if we do not know which context is causing the man's physique, we will be unable to decide which course of action to take. Essentially, we would need to guess what to do.

Returning our focus to learning improvement efforts, the collection of baseline performance data must be interpreted in light of the baseline context. The goal of this step is to investigate both current student performance (baseline performance) and the current learning context that fostered this level of performance (the baseline environment). This information is then integrated and used to focus the intervention development process as well as to detect whether the intervention changes were actually improvements.

Recall from the example in chapter 2 that Xela and Rusty worked with their colleagues to collect baseline data about students' ability to write appropriately in different contexts. Using a multiple-choice test and two performance assessments, they tested seniors nearing graduation and found poor performance across all measures. Table 6.1 displays the performance of senior students during the 1st year of the improvement initiative. The students represented in the table had experienced the baseline learning environment. In other words, they did not receive any of the new curricular elements that were developed during the learning improvement initiative.

Furthermore, when they explored the current learning environment, only one instructor reported covering audience-appropriate writing in class. With a single exception, the learning environment was devoid of interventions targeting the SLOs. Of course, the process of evaluating baseline environments will vary in complexity. Some baseline environments may provide no instruction that targets the new outcomes, meaning that entirely new interventions will need to be introduced. Other baseline environments may address the SLOs to a minor degree, or they may address some aspects of the outcomes but not others. In these cases, accounting for current coverage of the SLOs requires a careful inventory of the current system. As we will discuss later in this chapter, some baseline environments may call for refinements to the current system rather than the creation of entirely new curricular elements.

TABLE 6.1
Assessment Data From Year 1

	Multiple choice (SLO 1)	Performance Assessments	
		Short answer (SLO 2)	Embedded assessment (SLO 3)
SLO covered	1	2	3
Average score for year 1 seniors	12.5/30	5.6/15	4.2/15

In this chapter, we will provide general guidelines for evaluating both baseline student performance and the baseline learning environment. Before we do so, however, we need to clarify some of the key terminology used in discussions of baseline performance measurement.

A Methodological Clarification: Value-Added Versus Learning Improvement

By now, the astute reader may be wondering about the difference between learning improvement and value-added approaches to assessment. By the 1980s, colleges had begun to grapple with ways to best evaluate the degree of change experienced by students as a function of attending college (Warren, 1984). In fact, this was the methodology advocated in the Spellings Commission's final report as a critical step in creating a more effective and transparent system of higher education (U.S. Department of Education, 2006). Rather than simply measuring a student's level of knowledge or ability upon graduation from college, value-added approaches also require measurement of knowledge or ability at the beginning of college. Both testing occasions should use the same measure so that the difference between the scores (known as a change score) can be calculated. This change score is assumed to reflect the value added to that student by their college attendance (Fulcher & Willse, 2007).

Learning improvement, however, focuses on changes in student learning at a very different level. When attempting to demonstrate learning improvement, the goal is to show that students in one graduating cohort display knowledge, skills, or abilities superior to those of a previous graduating cohort. Additionally, we hope to gather evidence that improved student skills are due to a better learning environment. While information about students' abilities at entry to the program is useful (particularly when there is reason to believe that adjacent cohorts might have different levels of ability or skill at entry), it is not necessary for demonstrating learning improvement. Cross-sectional data collection processes can be appropriately applied when evaluating changes in program efficacy.

To demonstrate the difference between value-added methods and the learning improvement approach, imagine the following scenario. A biology program assesses its students when they first declare the biology major and again a few weeks prior to their graduation. A faculty member compares the scores and finds that students, on average, score a 75 at pretest and an 80 at posttest. From a value-added perspective, the efficacy of the program is now a +5. In other words, the students' scores were consistently improving about 5 points from the time they entered the program to the time they left. However, these data provide no evidence that program-level learning improvement has occurred. In Table 6.2, we can see this pattern in the class of 2017 and the class of 2018.

A *program* improvement effort would require the faculty to agree that a 5-point change is insufficient. The department would need to make intentional, coordinated changes to the learning environment so that students, on average, would score more than 80 points at posttest, even though the pretest average will likely remain around 75 points. This pattern is demonstrated in the class of 2019 and class of 2020 in Table 6.2. Students graduating in the class of 2019 were exposed to a partially revised learning environment, and their change score (+15 on average) is greater than that experienced by previous cohorts. This pattern is even more dramatic for the class of 2020, who received the curricular modifications experienced by the class of 2019 in addition to other new curricular modifications. This graduating class had an average change score of +20. Learning improvement, then, has occurred for both the class of 2019 and the class of 2020.

Given the appropriate assessment apparatus, we assume most programs could show some degree of value added via consistently positive change scores. Nevertheless, consistently positive change scores do not mean that the program has improved every year. As illustrated by the previous example, the program's efficacy in 2017 and 2018 was essentially the same: In both years, change scores were, on average, +5. We may thus consider a change score of +5 as a baseline change score to which future cohorts would be compared. This allows us to identify the improvement that occurred for the

TABLE 6.2
**Assessment Data, Learning Environments, Change Scores,
and Learning Improvement Status Across Four Cohorts**

| Cohort | Mean Score | | Learning Environment | Change Score | Learning Improvement |
	Pretest	Posttest			
Class of 2017	75	80	Same as the previous year	+5	No
Class of 2018	75	80	Same as the previous year	+5	No
Class of 2019	75	90	Partially revised from previous year	+15	Yes
Class of 2020	75	95	Revisions from the previous year plus new modifications	+20	Yes

classes of 2019 and 2020, which demonstrated much higher change scores than the previous cohorts. In other words, the average amount of change from program entry to program exit increased.

In our experience in higher education, comparisons of change scores are rarely used when evidencing improvement. Methodologically, this approach is extremely difficult to execute. It requires testing multiple students at multiple times, using the same measures at both time points, and being able to match the students at pretest and posttest to determine how much each student has gained. Because of these difficulties, most learning improvement projects assume similarity of knowledge and skill across cohorts in adjacent years (or, more specifically, across a 2- to 4-year span). Of course, this assumption will not be reasonable in all contexts. When there is reason to believe that students might have different levels of knowledge or skill at entry to the program, gathering pretest data is a crucial step. Once again, these methodological considerations underscore the importance of consulting with an assessment expert during learning improvement projects.

Instead, in the learning improvement examples we have seen, a cross-sectional data collection approach is typically employed. For example, a program will assess multiple cohorts of seniors. They first assess the cohort that received the "old" learning environment to evaluate the baseline performance of the program. Then, as changes to the learning environment are implemented, subsequent cohorts of graduating seniors are assessed to determine how different doses of the new learning environment relate to student achievement upon graduation. By "doses," we mean degrees of implementation of the new curriculum experienced by the students. For example, recall that two cohorts in Table 6.2 displayed learning improvement: The class of 2019 achieved an average change score of +15, which increased to +20 for the class of 2020. Imagine that the biology program's substantial changes affected one course taken during students' junior year and two courses taken during students' senior year. Even if both modifications are implemented for the first time during the 2018–2019 school year, students graduating in 2019 will only experience the modifications to the course taken during their senior year. In other words, they will receive only a partial dose of the new learning environment. The next cohort (class of 2020) will have received the full dosage, experiencing the modifications to the junior-year course and the two senior-year courses. This cross-sectional comparison of three graduating senior cohorts is what is used to determine if the changes to the learning environment resulted in the improvement of student learning.

Aside from these technical details, it is worth remembering that the purpose of these endeavors is to help students improve on the knowledge and skill sets we find important. At the heart of these methodological considerations is the pursuit of useful changes that will benefit students. We encourage our readers to remember this throughout this book: The purpose is always to better serve our students. Rigorous research methods are simply a tool (and, then, only *one* of the necessary tools) to achieve that goal.

Evaluating Baseline Student Performance

In chapter 5, we argued that well-developed test items are the clearest possible operationalization of vision. Good assessment tasks or items elicit behaviors from students indicating the degree to which they have achieved the intended SLOs, which have been established to reflect the initiative's vision. High scores on the measure generally indicate that students are closer to realizing the vision of student learning, while low scores suggest the opposite. Therefore, we noted the importance of using an assessment tool that is closely aligned to the SLOs. The tool may be an already-existing measure that matches the program's SLOs well, or it may be a new measure developed by the program. In either case, using the right instrument is a critical component in evidencing learning improvement.

We noted in chapter 2 that an assessment measure should not be changed once baseline data have been collected. Inevitably, participants in the learning improvement process will discover elements of the measure they dislike as the improvement effort progresses. Understandings of the construct will evolve throughout the learning improvement process, and this will likely result in some degree of friction against the chosen measure. Measurement tools are necessarily imperfect reflections of complex constructs (although readers are encouraged to contact the authors if they happen to find a measure that perfectly reflects an outcome and obtains universal agreement from all involved stakeholders). However, it is of critical importance that the same measure is used at all measurement points. As we have mentioned in prior chapters, measurement of change requires stability of the measure. If changes are made to the measure between uses, then it is difficult or impossible to tell whether score changes result from the measure modifications or from changes in students' ability or knowledge. If proper care has been taken in evaluating the measure in the first place, the instrument will at least be good enough (even if not perfect) to evaluate the effectiveness of the new learning environment. However, if the measure is adjusted or outright abandoned, the ability to compare student performance to that of the baseline cohort evaporates.

Because a strong coalition has been established at the beginning of the process, faculty will likely be open to collaborating in the collection of baseline data. There are two main options for data collection: requiring student participation in a special testing session or embedding the data collection process in courses. While the course-embedded approach may be helpful in increasing examinee effort (and, therefore, may result in more accurate estimates of baseline student performance), it also requires the use of valuable class time. Similarly, while the establishment of a required testing session avoids the use of class time, it risks lower examinee effort (Ewell, 2009). It is unlikely that both options will be equally feasible in all contexts, so the choice of approach should be chosen based on logistical and practical considerations. As in many other testing decisions, we recommend consulting an assessment professional for help weighing the benefits of each option. Whichever approach is chosen, the program must stick with this data collection methodology throughout the learning improvement process.

Evaluating the Baseline Learning Environment

Generating a clear picture of the baseline learning environment requires a careful approach to data collection. The goal of this process is to understand how the current learning environment seeks to address the target SLOs (or, perhaps, to determine whether the current learning environment addresses the SLOs at all). Studying the baseline learning environment will likely require a great deal of collaboration with faculty members across the program, and a culture of trust and mutual respect is a necessary precursor to gathering useful information. At this point in the process, lack of coverage cannot be seen as a failure; instead, it must be viewed as an opportunity for growth.

A key component of the evaluation process is the creation of a curriculum map (Jankowski & Marshall, 2017). Curriculum maps identify the places in the academic program where faculty intend to cover specified concepts or skills. The process of mapping a curriculum provides useful information about the way student knowledge is expected to progress through the course of the program, but it can also expose broken links. As frustrating as these discoveries may be, they provide crucial information for learning improvement initiatives by identifying opportunities for more intentionally linked programming.

Collecting Baseline Learning-Environment Information: Simple Example

To illustrate the evaluation of a baseline learning environment, we will revisit and expand on Rusty and Xela's experiences. Initially, the pair examined the original SLOs and curriculum map. The initial writing SLO (prior to the learning improvement initiative) read

> Students graduating from the Psychology BA program will be able to effectively write research articles, including introduction, methodology, results, and discussion sections.

They examined the program's curriculum map (see Table 6.3), which indicated where the SLO was intended to be introduced (I), reinforced (R,), and mastered (M).

Xela and Rusty's new idea of contextually aligned writing was a significant departure from the original writing SLO. Nevertheless, the original curriculum map gave them an idea of where writing skills were emphasized. Furthermore, if anyone was addressing contextually aligned writing, chances were that person would be among the faculty teaching these courses.

Xela and Rusty had a conversation with the faculty teaching the courses in which writing was emphasized. Almost all the instructors had noticed issues with contextual mismatches in their students' writing. Further, most of the instructors said they mainly focused on teaching students how to write a standard, American Psychological Association (APA)–style research report. There was a single exception: One faculty member, Ali, mentioned that his course briefly covered the differences between research reports and other genres.

Xela and Rusty met with him to gather more information early in the intervention development process. Ali explained that he had graded far

TABLE 6.3
SLO Coverage by Course

Course	Coverage
Introductory Psychology	-
Introductory Research Methods	I
Cognitive Psychology	R
Social Psychology	R
Abnormal Psychology	-
Careers in Psychology	-
Advanced Psychological Statistics	-
Capstone	M

too many research papers written with inappropriately informal language. Eventually, he became so frustrated that he created an in-class project to help students see the difference between the type of writing he often received and the level of formality he desired. He handed out sample paragraphs (modeled after real student research reports) that used inappropriately informal language. Students were asked to rewrite the paragraphs to better fit the formal style of a published study, which they then shared with a partner during a peer critique session. Ali noted that he regularly referred students back to this exercise when they needed additional help refining their style, occasionally running through his small archive of sample paragraphs with struggling students during his office hours.

While the instructor's intervention was relatively short (one class), he was thinking along the same lines as Xela and Rusty. Upon noticing a problem, he made explicit to students what was appropriate and what was not. Further, he created an activity that allowed students to practice the skill and receive peer feedback. This was the kind of person that Xela and Rusty wanted in their inner circle of implementers: someone invested in the process of improving student writing ability.

When a relatively new skill is the target of a learning improvement effort, the "current curriculum" will be (more or less) a blank slate. Although a few isolated examples of coverage—like Ali's in-class activity—may be evident, the evaluation of the baseline learning environment will find little to no coordinated effort to address the identified problem. This represents a fairly simple understanding of the baseline: No one focused on the SLO, so no one taught in a way that could be expected to change achievement on the SLO. Other cases, though, may be more complicated.

Collecting Baseline Learning-Environment Information: A More Complicated Example

Imagine if the program had made some steps in the past to address context-aligned writing. Perhaps they had selected a program-level SLO like the following:

> Students graduating from the Psychology BA program will know how to execute various writing styles common to the field of psychology.

Imagine, too, that the program had taken steps toward meeting this outcome, but that the efforts had been largely disconnected from each other. A learning improvement initiative was then launched with the more specific SLOs we've discussed throughout this book:

Upon graduating from the psychology program, students will

- recognize the elements of a writing context that influence appropriate choice of writing strategy;
- explain the reasons for differences among written communication styles relevant to psychological research, scientific communication, and professional workplaces; and
- demonstrate the ability to write about the same content for a number of different audiences, purposes, and occasions.

In this case, an evaluation of the baseline learning environment would not be likely to turn up a "blank slate." Because the old and new SLOs reflect similar ideas, we would likely see interventions across the program that somewhat reflect the aims of the improvement initiative. We may find, though, that these interventions are not intentionally connected to each other or that they do not reflect a common vision. Rather than introducing novel curricular elements intended to address a new skill, then, these sorts of improvement initiatives could more aptly be described as refinement processes. Collecting baseline learning-environment data is more complicated in such situations. Although coverage of the construct is widespread, the variability is likely to be immense. Therefore, painting a clear picture of the current learning environment will likely take more time than if the program had never addressed the construct at all.

When facing this sort of scenario, the need for alterations to the curriculum may not be immediately clear. Faculty may believe the old curriculum satisfactorily addresses the new SLOs. Therefore, it is imperative to make the disconnect between the curriculum and the new SLOs visible, which requires focusing faculty's attention on the existing variability in the program. Are all students in a position to achieve the specified SLOs? Or does individual student success depend on which course sections they happen to complete? A unified approach to learning improvement—one that spans an entire academic program—requires close consideration of this variability in order to move forward.

We recommend setting up a separate meeting for each relevant course. Invite all faculty who regularly teach that course to attend, and ask each person to bring all course materials related to the old SLO. First, have them describe the course materials or lessons they brought. Collect information about the time each element takes to implement, the goals of the lessons or materials, and any additional details that the instructor thinks are important to understanding their contribution. Then, map the interventions to the new SLOs. Prompt them to be courteous, collaborative, and critical. Remind them that the purpose is to improve student learning and that improvement will require change. After the meeting, evaluate the information you have collected. Are there consistent strategies being used within each course, or does each instructor take a radically different approach? What are the typical interventions a given student would experience as they move through the program? Would you expect each student to have generally similar experiences, or would their exposure to interventions targeting the outcome vary widely depending on their particular course sequence and set of instructors?

To make this process more concrete, let's imagine that a curriculum map suggests that two courses emphasize context-aligned writing (PSYC 290 and PSYC 360) in our new hypothetical program. Each course has three sections, each taught by a different faculty member. The program has already committed to a learning improvement initiative, so the faculty are willing participants. Table 6.4 displays a sample of the resulting information. The first column lists each of the course sections and their respective instructors. The remaining columns identify each of the new SLOs. The cells in the body of the table indicate which interventions (if any) in the section target each SLO.

All three PSYC 290 instructors assigned students a set of readings on APA style that provided some rationale for the style of social science research reports. All three instructors also devoted a full class meeting to a discussion about the differences between research report writing and other types of writing they have experienced. In total, students receive about 5 hours of intervention between the readings and the class discussion. All three instructors agreed that the in-class discussion most closely aligned to the SLO. However, the exercise did not explicitly contrast the types of writing relevant to psychological research, scientific communication, and professional workplaces; instead, it focused mainly on the APA-style research report and how the form differs from the five-paragraph essays the students likely used in high school. No explicit instruction was provided about writing in the workplace, scientific communication, or any other forms of writing that students might need to master in the future. In sum, the class discussion was more closely related to the SLO than any other element of the curriculum, but it did not match the SLO perfectly.

The three PSYC 360 sections displayed a different pattern. Two of the three sections delivered an assignment that was closely matched with the third SLO component. Valerie and Karen both used an assignment requiring students to rewrite one of their existing research papers into a newspaper article. Students were provided with readings about adapting scientific research for a general, nonscientific audience to guide their process. Valerie and Karen acknowledged, though, that this represented the only content translation

TABLE 6.4
Interventions Mapped to SLOs

	SLO 1: Recognize the elements of a writing context that influence appropriate choice of writing strategy	SLO 2: Explain the reasons for differences among written communication styles relevant to psychological research, scientific communication, and professional workplaces	SLO 3: Demonstrate the ability to write about the same content for a number of different audiences, purposes, and occasions
PSYC 290.1 (Janice)	-	Students are assigned a set of readings about APA style. Early in the semester, the class discusses the differences between research writing and other forms of writing (5 total hours of intervention).	-
PSYC 290.2 (JoAnne)	-		-
PSYC 290.3 (Steven)	-		-
PSYC 360.1 (David)	-	-	-
PSYC 360.2 (Valerie)	-	-	Assignment in class requiring students to rewrite their research paper for the local newspaper (10 total hours of intervention).
PSYC 360.3 (Karen)	-	-	

exercise in their courses. David, who did not implement the assignment in his section, noted that his class fell behind schedule this year. Although he usually uses the same content translation assignment, he had to abandon it in order to catch the class up.

After examining the table, the faculty concluded that current coverage of the new SLOs was inconsistent and insufficient. None of their courses corresponded to SLO 1. PSYC 290 covered different writing styles (the core of SLO 2), and students did have to explain them. Nevertheless, the material covered in the readings and class discussion did not fully address the SLO. Similarly, SLO 3 was underrepresented in PSYC 360. The assignments for sections 360.2 and 360.3 required only one type of rewrite (from research paper to newspaper article) whereas the SLO asks students to "write about the same content for a number of different audiences, purposes, and occasions." Last, one faculty member, David, did not cover the outcome at all in his section. In sum, the faculty realized that the learning environment would need to be modified substantially in order for students to meet the SLOs.

Closing Thoughts

In combination, the two types of baseline data are powerful. Not only will this information lend learning improvement teams a sense of students' current level of proficiency, but it will also provide a firm understanding of the learning environment associated with the observed level of proficiency. These pieces of information collectively position the program well to make informed, strategic changes to the learning environment.

Exercises

1. What is the difference between a value-added approach to assessment and learning improvement? What are the methodological consequences of this distinction?
2. What are performance baseline data and learning-environment baseline data? Why is it critical to study both in tandem?
3. Identify or create a simple, nonacademic example of highlighting the relationship between performance and learning-environment baseline data.
4. For an academic program, create hypothetical performance and learning-environment baseline data in tandem. Describe the performance data in the context of the learning environment data.

7

DEVELOPING
INTERVENTIONS

The development of effective interventions is one of the most important and time-consuming parts of the learning improvement process. This process benefits from the use of discipline-specific scholarship of teaching and learning, as well as literature from cognition and the learning sciences. This chapter outlines some basic concepts from these disciplines, along with an example of how these sources of information can be combined to plan interventions.

Chapter 6 described the steps necessary for evaluating a program's baseline in terms of student performance as well as the educational context. It is worth remembering that the purpose of this baseline evaluation is to inform change efforts. Without making changes to the educational environment, we would not expect to see better learning outcomes. In this chapter, we outline the process of developing interventions that can bring about student learning improvement.

Recall that the simple model of improvement includes three steps: assess, intervene, and reassess. A surface-level interpretation of this model may indicate that only a third of the learning improvement process depends on the chosen interventions, with the remaining emphasis placed on assessment methods. However, as we have noted elsewhere (Fulcher & Prendergast, 2019), a more accurate representation of the model would likely show the "intervene" step in towering letters, sandwiched by two smaller references to assessment (Figure 7.1).

While high-quality assessment is an integral part of learning improvement, the development and implementation of strong interventions are likely to require far more time, resources, and faculty involvement than the development and implementation of assessment techniques. Interventions are the

Figure 7.1. Proportional relationship of intervention to assessment in improvement efforts.

Assess, Intervene, Reassess

heart of learning improvement, and assessment processes play a supporting role by framing and evaluating those interventions.

Therefore, there are two major stages of the intervention phase that need careful attention: developing interventions and implementing interventions. In the first stage, the goal is to devise learning-environment changes intended to improve student learning. The goal of the second stage is to translate those planned interventions into action by integrating them into the educational context. In this chapter, we will be focusing on intervention development. Chapter 8 will address how to implement the newly developed interventions.

Interventions: What Are They?

An intervention is an action, program, tool, or technique that is intended to improve an outcome. Interventions take very different forms in different contexts, and an adequate intervention to improve one outcome is likely to be wholly inadequate for the purpose of improving another outcome. One of our colleagues often uses a fitness metaphor to introduce the idea of interventions. Simply put, exercising is the intervention meant to bring about better fitness outcomes. As in learning, however, the devil is in the details. What exact fitness outcomes are we trying to achieve? Where are we starting from? And, what types of exercises (interventions)—under what conditions—are most effective at increasing these specific fitness outcomes?

Imagine a group of runners who dream of running a great distance across considerable elevation change. Their full articulation of this vision is to run a mountain half marathon, which is 4 months away. While all members of the group have some running experience, they are not currently prepared to run the mountain half marathon. Currently, each person runs about 10 to 15 miles a week. Three-mile runs are typical, and 6 miles on any given day is about as far as any of them can run. All of the runners are used to training on flat trails.

They compared their current levels of fitness and workout routines to their goal of a mountain half marathon. They would undoubtedly need to work on the following two areas to be successful:

- Distance (need to be able to run 13.1 miles)
- Incline running (need to be comfortable running long stretches of steep inclines)

How would they achieve these goals? They consulted the literature. Useful information was plentiful. Olympic runners, professional coaches, exercise physiologists, and other experts had shared their training strategies. Considerably less literature was available that specifically addressed half-marathon mountain runs, but the readings on both half-marathons and running in steep terrain were numerous.

Across these readings, the runners realized they would need to gradually increase their weekly mileage from 10 to about 25 miles over the next 4 months. Each week would have one long run, which would eventually need to reach 10 miles. They also need to incorporate cross-training, recovery, and incline work into their weekly regimen. After investigating several plans, they settled on a training plan to use as their base. They tweaked the plan to include more hill work in order to account for the mountainous setting of their impending half marathon.

Table 7.1 compares the runners' interventions from their current habits and ability level to their vision for achieving a new goal. The changes they wish to make are operationalized via the difference between their current and aspiring performance level. The exercise regimen offers the pathway between their current status and their goal.

Note the juxtaposition of the group's current and aspirational performance levels and their exercise regimens. The table illuminates several relationships. It is clear that the current performance level is being supported by

TABLE 7.1
Current and Aspiring Performance Levels and Exercise Regimens

	Current	*Aspiring*
Performance level	The runners typically can run a maximum of about 6 miles on a flat surface.	The runners can complete a mountain half marathon (13.1 miles).
Exercise regimen	Three runs per week, each typically about 3 to 4 miles long. The runs take place on relatively flat trails.	A scaffolded running regimen over the course of 16 weeks, starting from 10 miles per week and ending at about 25 miles per week. The exercise plan consists of one long run per week, three or four shorter runs, cross-training, hill running, and a recovery day.

the current exercise environment; the most likely reason the group can run a maximum of 6 miles is because they currently run three times a week, 3 to 4 miles at a time. Moving to the vision of running a half marathon requires a shift in desired performance level accompanied by an augmented exercise regimen.

Imagine if their "aspiring" regimen was not aligned with the performance goal. Let us provide two extreme examples. Perhaps the runners abandoned their current routine and began working only on their upper bodies through push-ups, dips, and bench presses. These exercises, while worthwhile for other purposes, are unlikely to help the group run a longer distance over mountainous terrain. Alternatively, the group may have decided that they would watch several videos of people running marathons. Again, this is not a bad idea, but would watching videos of people running actually improve their performance? Unlikely. These examples illustrate that not all interventions are effective; in fact, in some cases, they can be detrimental. For example, abandoning the current running regimen in favor of upper body exercises likely will put greater distance between the runners and their vision. The key is changing the exercise in a way that produces the desired outcome.

Another concern is the underpowered intervention. In the example in Table 7.1, note the dramatic increase from the current exercise regimen to the aspiring regimen. The runners are to gradually increase their running from 10 miles per week to 25. Imagine, alternatively, that the new exercise regimen only called for runners to peak at 12 miles per week. The intervention is on the right track, but underpowered. It is unlikely that a 2-mile-per-week increase will prepare the runners to complete the half marathon.

How is this relevant to higher education? We think of "intervening" as making changes in the learning environment to improve student learning. The difference in effectiveness between the current learning environment and the new learning environment is the mechanism for learning improvement. Much like the runners change their mileage and adjust their workouts, educators introduce or modify curriculum and pedagogical techniques within their program. And like the aspiring marathon runners, educators have a wealth of available resources related directly to their work.

Consulting the Literature

Knowledge of the literature is important for all stages of the learning improvement process, but it is perhaps most crucial to the development of effective interventions. As with all other forms of scholarly work, we benefit from standing on the shoulders of those who came before us. Two types of literature are useful in guiding the development of interventions: literature within a particular discipline (e.g., the scholarship of teaching and learning in the field of psychology) and literature from the cognitive and learning sciences (e.g., research investigating techniques to improve college students' metacognitive awareness). Key lessons from the latter field will be discussed later in this chapter.

The discipline-specific literature is particularly helpful in fields with a tradition of scholarship of teaching and learning. As noted by Dickson and Treml (2013), the scholarship of teaching and learning is often driven by a focus on individual courses within specific disciplines. People leading program-level improvement initiatives can and should examine this research. The methods described therein may be well positioned to become program-level interventions if they can be scaled across the curriculum. Dickson and Treml (2013) urged faculty to integrate rigorous data collection, analysis, and reflection into their efforts to improve course-level teaching strategies. Doing so (and publishing the results) represents a move from "scholarly teaching" to full engagement in the scholarship of teaching and learning. We call on faculty to take one ambitious step further: Using scholarship as a guide, we call for coordinated, program-wide efforts to find or develop theoretically informed teaching interventions.

Unfortunately, not all SLOs will be well aligned with a rich body of existing literature. If the outcome targeted by the learning improvement initiative is not well represented in the research, a different literature base can be consulted. Cognitive and learning sciences can inform various interventions, regardless of discipline. Our institution, for example, has spent years developing students' ethical reasoning skills. Because the framework for ethical reasoning was locally developed, there was no existing disciplinary literature base from which to guide our interventions (although theories on ethical reasoning itself were instrumental to the process). However, we found support in the literature on decision-making and cognitive processing (Sanchez et al., 2017). The content experts leading the initiative theorized that students' poor ethical reasoning skills were largely due to the tendency to make quick decisions and then justify them later. Therefore, the team began examining research on decision-making and methods to alter decision-making patterns. Behavioral economist Daniel Kahneman's (2011) research on slowing automatic cognitive processes to enhance decision-making, for example, was used in the development of ethical reasoning interventions.

Despite the benefits of grounding initiative development in existing literature, we have seen many faculty members depend on intuition and instinct when developing interventions. Of course, many of these academics are quite clever, and many have a good sense of students' needs. It is unsurprising, then, for them to expect they could invent effective interventions without reviewing additional literature. Certainly, we would anticipate that some interventions developed this way would lead to successful learning improvement projects. However, researchers around the world have spent untold hours cumulatively studying interventions related to a massive array of educational topics and skills. Why not take the time to learn from this work from the beginning of the intervention development stage? Why not combine lessons from the literature with lessons from instructors' experiences and wisdom?

Discipline-Specific Literature

Faculty will often be most comfortable beginning with the literature within their field's scholarship of teaching and learning (SoTL). Many disciplines have a rich tradition of turning a scholarly eye to pedagogy (Huber & Morreale, 2002), and conferences and journals devoted to disciplinary SoTL abound. These resources can be helpful prior to the development of interventions, as they may help solidify understandings of key constructs. By examining how others have set about defining and studying the knowledge, skills, and abilities of their students, we can begin to refine our own definitions of those constructs.

An obvious benefit of discipline-specific literature is that the research context is familiar to the reader. This relatability often makes such research findings easily applicable to new classroom settings (e.g., those of the faculty in the intervention chain of a learning improvement initiative). Additionally, it allows us to live vicariously through the labor and mistakes of those before us: What interventions have worked elsewhere? What measures were used to evaluate the intervention's success? How were the interventions developed? What resources were needed for their implementation? These questions (and more) can save time in the development of new or adapted interventions, and they can spur ideas that may not arise without outside influence. A close examination of unsuccessful interventions is also likely to be useful in planning curricular changes. Just as a report of a successful new intervention can identify techniques worth trying, reports of ineffective interventions can identify techniques worth avoiding. Each of these types of information can save precious time and energy.

We recommend, then, that the champions of the learning improvement initiative identify SoTL resources (journals, electronic mailing lists, websites, and conferences) early in the planning process. Engaging with this literature on a regular basis will provide new ideas for interventions, new resources for instructors, and new approaches to assessment of student learning. Importantly, the team leading the learning improvement attempt should plan to eventually contribute their own work to the discipline's SoTL body. Continued successful attempts at learning improvement will be fostered if effective interventions are assessed rigorously and reported in the literature. Your contributions at the conclusion of a learning improvement initiative may very well lay the groundwork for another program's efforts.

Cognition and Learning Science

A great deal of SoTL literature depends heavily on research in cognition and the learning sciences. Therefore, the distinction we draw here between discipline-specific literature and cognition and learning science literature is somewhat contrived. However, it is important to note that useful information that can help guide intervention development can be found outside of SoTL resources. Entire fields have devoted themselves to the study of learning, and a rich body of research exists on how best to structure education to facilitate enduring learning. Consulting this body of knowledge will be particularly useful when little existing research is available for the construct at the center of the learning improvement initiative. In other words, if you need to build an intervention from scratch, you will likely want some guidance from experts in cognition and learning.

Although the literature in cognition and the learning sciences can be difficult to understand without a background in psychology or education, several accessible resources translate this work and show how it can be applied to college programs. For example, Halpern and Hakel (2003) provide an excellent overview of learning science principles that can and should be applied to college classrooms.

They argue that the main goal of college instruction is to facilitate two things: long-term retention and the transfer of learning to new situations and contexts. Attention to these goals when designing educational interventions can facilitate recall and application of knowledge and skills long after a student completes a final exam or receives a diploma. Although this list was published nearly 2 decades ago, its major principles (summarized in the following list) can still be considered useful guidelines for intervention development:

1. "Practice at retrieval," or repeatedly accessing knowledge under different circumstances and in different contexts, can increase the fluency with which the information can be retrieved in the future. An intervention

integrating this principle might look like repeatedly quizzing students on the knowledge they have accumulated across a semester or across a course sequence.

2. Learning in varied conditions, while more difficult than in static conditions, results in better learning. For example, interventions with varied conditions for learning may require students to apply new concepts in several different ways, supporting students as they struggle through the inevitable confusion. A math professor might introduce a calculus formula in a simple format, and then give students various word problems that require that formula, sometimes with extraneous information. While often frustrating for students, navigating such problems in messy contexts is more like what students will experience after college.

3. Students are likely to learn better when required to translate information from one format into another. A common application of this principle is the concept map: Students may be asked to read a chapter or listen to a presentation and then create a map displaying the relationships among key concepts.

4. Prior knowledge and experience impact the quantity and quality of learning. If students do not understand fundamental concepts at the beginning of a complicated lesson, they will likely be unable to extract as much meaning from the lesson as they would if their prior knowledge was higher. This, of course, has important implications for evaluation of baseline learning environments (does the current environment prepare students for upper-level courses?). Interventions incorporating this principle might include "refresher" modules referencing introductory-level materials at the beginning of upper-level courses.

5. Student and instructor epistemologies affect student learning. For example, students who associate the feeling of struggling while learning with failure may be less likely to persist through difficult topics than students who embrace the struggle. Interventions emphasizing growth mindset, for example, can help students to develop epistemologies that are more supportive of learning.

6. Learning from experience alone can easily lead us astray, and confidence in mastery of a topic does not necessarily correspond to actual knowledge. It is therefore important to receive regular feedback about our knowledge, skills, and abilities. Interventions that provide frequent formative assessments, then, can be useful for preventing solidification of erroneous beliefs.

7. Lectures are typically not the best choice for facilitating conceptual understanding, and the typical multiple-choice test may mask issues with

deeper learning. More effective approaches include techniques like inter-teaching or flipped classrooms.

8. Students forget what they are not asked to recall. Alternatively, they tend to retain the information they have been required to remember. Interventions that facilitate regular recall of important concepts, then, can be expected to facilitate long-term memory of those concepts. As Halpern and Hakel (2003) note, this effect is strengthened when a longer period of time is allowed to pass between the time of initial learning and the time of testing.

9. Individual courses can achieve breadth or depth of content coverage, but typically not both. A focus on depth, though, is likely to be more effective in the long term than a focus on covering an excessively broad range of concepts. Interventions stemming from this principle might include restructuring introductory or foundational courses to develop a deeper understanding of the discipline's key principles rather than broad survey knowledge. Fink (2013) speaks to this point as well. Often, courses are organized based on topics (demonstrating a "breadth" approach). Fink argues they should be organized around skills. Or, in other words, courses should place skills in the foreground and content in the background. This point should not be misinterpreted as knowledge being unimportant, but rather that knowledge should be put in the service of skills (e.g., historical facts can be developed in the service of critical thinking).

10. What students remember after a course concludes is largely dependent on what those students are asked to do during the course. This principle calls for the use of interventions that require students to actively engage with information (e.g., through lessons guided by the preceding nine principles) in order to facilitate long-term retention and transfer.

These 10 guiding principles are deceptively simple, and their implications for planning interventions are immense. Their most alluring attribute, though, is their broad-ranging applicability: We would argue that any course covering any topic anywhere in the country could benefit from application of these principles. Another useful introduction to learning sciences principles is Matlin's (2002) annotated bibliography of resources on cognitive psychology resources for faculty members. This article covers general frameworks, research on memory and metamemory, text comprehension and metacomprehension, writing, attention, multimedia, and testing, among others.

Resources such as these can provide a helpful foundation for the development of effective interventions. Faculty members by nature have a thorough understanding of knowledge within their discipline; however, most graduate programs do not prepare future college instructors for the challenges of teaching for long-term retention and transfer to novel situations. This should not be seen as a shortcoming of college instructors, but as an excellent reason to become acquainted with the literature in the learning sciences.

Combining the Two: An Example

Ideally, the champions of the learning improvement initiative will have ample disciplinary literature to draw from in addition to research in cognition and learning sciences. Stitching these pieces together then becomes the next step in developing a plan for changing the learning environment. Recall from chapter 2 that Xela and Rusty drew from both sources when developing new interventions to address students' context-aligned writing skills. They first turned their attention to the literature soon after the core team for the initiative was assembled. Later, they returned to the literature with the assistance of Ida, the faculty developer, as they began to plan new course interventions to target their outcomes. Also recall that the interventions before that point were essentially nonexistent. Therefore, any new interventions would amount to a differential shift in the learning environment relative to the SLO.

The core group spent a month poring over the literature. They met weekly to discuss what they learned. While they searched for literature on teaching context-aligned writing in psychology programs, they were unable to find any examples of published research that addressed the department's specific concerns. However, Xela and her colleagues found substantial literature on other areas related to writing in undergraduate psychology programs. Although the interventions they reported did not perfectly align with the outcomes written for the learning improvement initiative, they did provide several ideas from which to begin building.

Feeling like they had a good handle on the literature, the core group scheduled two half-day meetings so they could develop the structure of their learning improvement initiative. What interventions would be created to help students with their aligned writing? How could these interventions be coordinated across the three designated courses? Their overall plan is outlined in Table 7.2. For now, we will focus on Intervention F, which is outlined in Table 7.3 (see Table 2.2 for further details on all interventions).

Xela and her colleagues incorporated a "cover letter" approach to the intervention in the capstone course, which requires students to provide a

TABLE 7.2
Introduction and Reinforcement of Outcomes by Course and Intervention

		SLO		
Course	*Intervention*	*1*	*2*	*3*
PSYC 201: Research Methods	A	I	I	
	B			I
PSYC 310: Careers in Psychology	C	R	R	
	D			R
PSYC 495: Capstone	E	R		
	F			R
	G			R

Note. I-introduced; R-reinforced

cover letter with each draft explaining their revisions and justifying stylistic choices. This approach, adapted from Daniel et al. (2015), was initially intended to improve students' ability to incorporate instructor feedback into successive drafts; however, Xela and her colleagues adapted the approach to focus on justification for stylistic choices in the paper. Their goal was

TABLE 7.3
Focus on Intervention F

Course	*Course Modifications*	*SLO Coverage*
PSYC 495: Capstone	**Intervention F:** The existing assignment for this course (producing a full scholarly research paper) was adapted to focus on the revision process. Previously, students turned in a single version of the research paper at the end of the semester. In the new version of the assignment, students turn in multiple drafts of each section of the paper (abstract, introduction, methods, results, and discussion) at specified points during the semester. In addition to each draft, students provide a cover letter detailing their revisions to previous versions of the draft (if relevant), provide justification for stylistic choices, and identify particular elements of their writing for which they would like to receive feedback.	SLO 3

to require students to explicitly reflect on the stylistic elements of the scholarly research paper, thereby drawing students' attention to the relationship between their writing and the demands of the context. Research on metacognition in writing (e.g., Sitko, 1998) indicated that this sort of explicit attention to the match between the writer's approach and the style of writing would help students become more aware of their choices and better able to evaluate their effectiveness. Table 7.4 displays the elements of the intervention—what we call "intervention features"—as well as planned time allotments for each of the intervention's components.

The approaches they took to developing interventions across courses also align with the general principles laid out by Halpern and Hakel (2003). For example, the new curricular elements require students to write for a variety of contexts, repackaging information for new audiences and occasions. This aligns with Halpern and Hakel's third principle, which states that students learn better through repeated translation of concepts into new formats. Additionally, the inclusion of multiple opportunities for students to receive feedback on their writing aligns with the sixth principle, which states that people can become overconfident in incorrect knowledge and abilities without regular feedback.

TABLE 7.4
Detailed Description of Intervention F

Intervention Feature	Planned Time
Students read about the genre of research papers in the social sciences.	1 hour
In-class discussion about the audience and purpose of the social scientific research paper.	1 hour
Students write a cover letter detailing the revisions to their introduction draft.	1 hour
Students write a cover letter detailing the revisions to their methods draft.	1 hour
Students write a cover letter detailing the revisions to their results draft.	1 hour
Students write a cover letter detailing the revisions to their discussion draft.	1 hour
Students write a cover letter detailing the revisions to their abstract draft.	1 hour

Note that Table 7.4 represents only one intervention (F) among seven, and from that single intervention students are to receive approximately 7 hours of exposure. There is no silver bullet for teaching students audience-aligned writing (or, likely, for anything else worth improving). It will take thoughtful, evidenced-based interventions that span considerable time to make a dent in students' knowledge and skills. This point is sometimes overlooked in the desire to implement programmatic changes: We have observed many institutions attempt to improve important skills with underpowered interventions. For instance, a single, 1-hour discussion on diversity—no matter how well executed—will not magically transform students into multicultural experts.

Another point about the interventions laid out in Tables 7.3 and 7.4 is that they are *planned* interventions at this stage. They have not yet been put into practice by the faculty teaching the courses. To do so, an implementation plan must be developed. Tracking intervention implementation is the focus of the next chapter.

In sum, the interventions developed by Rusty, Xela, and their team of colleagues integrated general learning science and cognition principles as well as research from the scholarship of teaching and learning in psychology. Although each of these elements, on their own, likely would have provided useful guidance in the development of new curricular elements, using both types of research together allowed them to be more confident that their proposed interventions would be effective.

Concluding Thoughts

Development of effective interventions is a difficult task, and often time consuming as well. In order to reasonably expect improvement at the program level, planned interventions need to represent a significant shift from current practices, they need to be well targeted to the outcomes that are the focus of the improvement initiative, and they need to be grounded in existing relevant literature. We discussed two main sources of literature that can provide guidance in intervention development: discipline-specific literature (specifically, the scholarship of teaching and learning) and cognition and learning science literature. Together, these sources can provide us with information about how students learn as well as how those before us have attempted to improve learning in their own classrooms. Of course, developing the interventions is only one half of the intervention process. In the next chapter we discuss considerations in implementing interventions at scale.

Exercises

1. Differentiate the roles of assessments and interventions in the learning improvement process.
2. From your own experience, describe examples of the following types of ineffective interventions:
   a. Misaligned interventions, where the nature of the intervention is unlikely to affect the desired outcome.
   b. Underpowered interventions, where the nature of the intervention should affect the desired outcome, but it is in too small of a "dose" to achieve the desired outcome.
3. Identify at least three journals in your field (or in an adjacent field) about teaching and learning. Find three articles that describe specific interventions. What evidence do the authors use to support the efficacy (or inefficacy) of these interventions?
4. Choose the intervention you liked best in exercise 3. Describe how it might be applied in your own program.
5. Halpern and Hakel (2003) make the argument that the ultimate goals of teaching are long-term retention and transfer. Think about an important concept in your field that you already teach.
   a. Why is it important that students retain the information long term?
   b. Why is it important that they can transfer the information/skills to novel settings?
   c. Provide specific examples of how you might teach that concept differently to promote long-term retention and transfer.

8

INTERVENTION
IMPLEMENTATION

Chapter 7 outlined the process of developing interventions, which are the changes in learning environments intended to produce better student learning. Intervention development, though, is only half the battle. Once a high-quality intervention has been developed, it needs to be implemented well for the learning environment to stand a chance of improvement. This chapter discusses essential considerations for implementation, including the central role of faculty, the importance of professional development, and the concept of implementation fidelity.

Faculty, Faculty, Faculty

If the three most important considerations for real estate are location, location, location, then the three most important considerations for intervention implementation are faculty, faculty, faculty. For well-designed, effective interventions to translate into improved student learning, they need to be implemented well. Faculty members are the primary conduit for the interventions. The key to success, then, is giving faculty time and space to adapt the interventions into their own classes, a task that benefits from the expertise and involvement of faculty developers. The expected relationship between faculty development and improved learning outcomes (Condon et al., 2016), as introduced in chapter 1, is as follows:

Step 1: Faculty member participates in professional development.
Step 2: Faculty member learns how to teach better.

Step 3: Faculty member integrates better teaching approach in course section(s).

Step 4: Students learn better as a function of the improved learning environment.

The spaces between knowing what works (step 2) and having those interventions reach students (step 3) in a way that results in improved learning (step 4) are vast. Therefore, providing high-quality professional development for faculty is a way to connect the dots between each of these steps.

Before diving deeper into implementation strategies, let us provide a cautionary tale. The first author once consulted with an institution attempting to improve critical thinking in 1st-year seminars. It was a university-level initiative that had a reasonable budget and support from senior leadership. An outside expert in critical thinking gave a 3-hour workshop to all faculty teaching the seminars. In the workshop, faculty were introduced to several evidence-based strategies for teaching critical thinking. After faculty members left the workshop, no further support for implementation was provided.

Did students' critical thinking skills improve because of their experience in 1st-year seminars?

Of course not.

There were serious problems with the implementation strategy. After a 3-hour workshop, was it plausible to believe that faculty would both master the concepts *and* know how to teach them? Even if they had, where would faculty find the dozens of hours necessary to reorganize their courses to include critical thinking interventions? In hindsight, the brief workshop-only format was grossly insufficient to prepare faculty for the important, challenging task of developing and integrating new interventions into their courses. For starters, courses are typically chock full of content, activities, and expectations prior to the development of a learning improvement project. Failing to provide time for faculty to integrate new interventions into existing, fully developed courses almost guarantees that the new interventions will never come to fruition. Careful attention and a good deal of time are therefore crucial for ensuring that the developed program components can be successfully integrated into existing course plans.

Fortunately, Xela and Rusty's strategy was much more coherent. They placed faculty at the heart of the process long before the implementation of the new interventions. In chapter 4, Xela and Rusty tested the waters with their colleagues to determine if colleagues had the collective will to improve context-appropriate writing. They did. From that point, the group of faculty—with several taking major leadership roles in the inner planning circle—articulated the vision for better writing (chapter 5), collected baseline data (chapter 6), and researched and developed evidence-based interventions designed to improve students' writing skills (chapter 7). Because of the extensive groundwork, when it was time to implement the interventions, all members of the intervention chain were familiar with (and approved of) the intervention plans. This was a group that was prepared and willing to change their learning environments.

The next part of Xela and Rusty's strategy was to provide the space and time for faculty to thoughtfully integrate the interventions into their own courses. All members of the intervention chain participated in a 3-day summer retreat. They planned the details of their interventions alongside Ida, the faculty development expert. They were provided with time and resources to adapt their existing courses in order to accommodate the new interventions. Each course group developed and agreed on an implementation fidelity plan (which will be discussed extensively later in this chapter).

During the 1st year of implementation, Xela and Rusty held monthly check-ins with the members of the intervention chain. These meetings served to provide feedback to the inner circle about how the interventions were being implemented, and they allowed members of the intervention chain to troubleshoot with their colleagues and adjust where needed.

Two Stages of Implementation

By this point in the learning improvement process, the inner circle is likely to have some ideas about the interventions that should be effective to improve student learning. They also have identified the courses in which these interventions should be delivered (chapter 7). The goal of implementation is to ensure that students experience the interventions as they were intended to be experienced. Implementation can be conceptualized as consisting of two important stages: preparing faculty to implement the intervention, and the delivery of the intervention itself.

When preparing faculty to implement interventions, success means that faculty are fully prepared to deliver the appropriate interventions in their courses. Specifically, after finishing their preparation, each instructor should

- know their course's specific role in the learning improvement project;
- be competent in the knowledge/skills they endeavor students to learn;
- understand the interventions for which they will be responsible for delivering;

- have a plan to integrate the interventions within their course sections; and
- if needed, customize the interventions to fit their style, preferences, and course context (while still maintaining the intervention's integrity).

We suggest that several days or more are set aside for this experience (a far cry from the 3-hour workshop we mentioned earlier). These experiences may be combined with professional development in other skills relevant to learning improvement initiatives, like planning assessment strategies. Faculty developers, like Ida, are often best suited to facilitate such sessions. Of course, the requirements of this stage are context specific. A learning improvement project that seeks to improve students' abilities in an area with which all faculty members are extremely familiar will require a different professional development process than if the area is new to most of the people involved. Several tools are helpful at this stage in the process, no matter the complexity of the project.

The first tool is a visual road map that provides a high-level overview of which interventions should be implemented in which courses (and by whom). This road map clarifies who is supposed to do what, and when they are to do it. It acts as a reminder of the overall strategy and that each team member is responsible for their part.

An example map is provided in Figure 8.1. The map represents three courses (201, 310, and 495), each of which are taught by five instructors. Each instructor is represented by a box labeled with their name, and each box lists the sections taught by that instructor (e.g., Rebecca teaches sections 9 and 10 of PSYC 201). The letters below the course sections identify the interventions added to each course. Rebecca's box indicates that she is responsible for implementing intervention A and B in her two sections of PSYC 201. Note that the other four PSYC 201 instructors are responsible for implementing these interventions in their sections as well. Details about each of these interventions are provided in Table 2.2 in chapter 2. Briefly, intervention A concerns the development of concept maps illustrating the features and purposes of various forms of scientific communication, while intervention B requires students to "translate" between different styles of scientific writing. This map displays the ideal state of the intervention implementation, with perfect horizontal alignment across sections of each course. A similar map could be created to demonstrate the use of specified interventions in the baseline learning environment, or to indicate partial implementation of an intervention during a pilot phase of the intervention development process. These alternative versions of the map are unlikely to demonstrate perfect alignment.

Figure 8.1. Visual representation of planned interventions, instructors, courses, and sections.

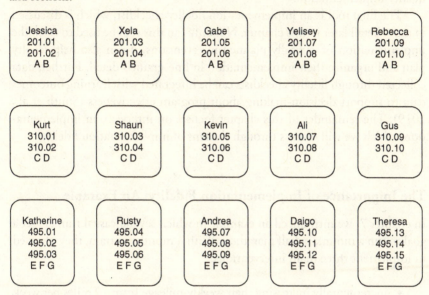

The second set of tools consists of exemplar activities, assignments, resources, and lessons that model possible additions to instructors' teaching repertoires. These exemplars are created by the inner circle and have been designed to specifically link to the project's SLOs. For many learning improvement projects, faculty are given the choice to modify these exemplars to best match the needs of their courses. Some may choose to keep the exemplars "as is," adopting a set of materials without making adjustments for their course. The flexibility of the exemplars will be highly dependent on the project at hand, the context, and the perspectives of the participating faculty members. But no matter whether the materials act as templates or final products, carefully designed exemplars greatly reduce the time it would take for all faculty members to create their materials from scratch.

The third tool is simple, but sometimes elusive: time. In a week-long professional development workshop, at least half the time (about 20 hours) should be set aside for faculty members to work on their part of the learning improvement initiative. As we noted earlier, faculty members must integrate and adapt interventions into their own sections. They often must reconsider and rearrange existing course content. Thus, they need time to workshop plans for new versions of their courses. Going into their own courses with much of the new material prepared greatly increases the probability of high-quality implementation.

The final tool is an implementation fidelity checklist, which is discussed in more detail later in this chapter. Not only can this tool be used to track the implementation of carefully planned interventions, it can also help faculty plan and organize their implementation in fine-grained detail. Further, data collected through fidelity checklists can be integrated with learning outcomes data to support decision-making about program effectiveness (Smith et al., 2019). The remainder of this chapter focuses on intervention implementation, which we will discuss through the lens of implementation fidelity.

The Importance of Implementation Fidelity: An Example

In chapter 7, we introduced an example in which several casual runners set a goal to run a mountain half marathon. With 4 months to train, they planned to implement three main interventions:

- incrementally increasing their weekly mileage from 10 miles per week to about 25 miles per week;
- incrementally increasing their longest run of the week from 3 miles to 10 miles; and
- integrating hills and other incline work into their routines.

Eventually, the day of the race arrived. With the bang of the starting pistol, the previously casual runners began the 13.1-mile race. By mile 4, one of the runners decided to drop out of the race. At mile 5, another runner quit. At mile 6, another tapped out. Only two of the five runners crossed the finish line. What went wrong? Why did only 40% of the running group manage to finish the race?

One reason might be the quality of the interventions. Recall that the team did not adopt obviously misaligned interventions like upper-body workouts or watching videos of runners. Nevertheless, it is possible the three-part plan was ineffective preparation for the half marathon despite being crafted based on expert advice. Perhaps it did not suit the needs of a mountainous course. The runners figured that the integration of hills and incline work into the existing half-marathon training program would be sufficient, but it is possible that this addition was inadequate. Perhaps if the race had been on a flatter route, their plan would have worked.

However, there is another possible explanation for why the training program did not result in a successful race for the whole team. Perhaps the runners simply did not implement the interventions as planned. What if one of the runners became too busy and maintained the old workout regimen of 10 miles per week, with a long run of 4 miles? What if another runner increased overall mileage but never reached the 10-mile goal for weekly long runs? These scenarios would not represent failures of intervention, but failures of implementation: The plan might have been perfectly effective, but the runners deviated dramatically from the plan.

Table 8.1 provides a summary of each runners' implementation fidelity—the degree to which they stuck to the training plan—and how they performed in the race. This table demonstrates the relationship between fidelity and race outcome: The runners exhibiting low fidelity dropped out, while the runners who stuck to the plan moderately or perfectly finished. Runner 5 increased her total mileage and the length of her long runs every week, and she completed the recommended incline work as planned. She managed to finish the race. Each of the other four runners displayed a mismatch between their behaviors and the training plan. The first and second runners adopted no elements of the new plan, while the third and fourth runners adopted only some of the plan. Runner 4 completed the race even though he had not followed the plan perfectly. Perhaps he was a gifted athlete, a more experienced runner, or simply lucky.

TABLE 8.1
Fidelity and Outcome for Each Runner

Runner	Fidelity to Intervention	Outcome
1	No elements of the new intervention; maintained old workout plan	Dropped out at mile 4
2	No elements of the new intervention; maintained old workout plan	Dropped out at mile 5
3	Low fidelity; increased weekly mileage but did not integrate hills; longest run of the week was 7 miles.	Dropped out at mile 6
4	Moderate fidelity; increased weekly mileage and integrated hills; longest run of the week was 7 miles.	Completed the half marathon
5	High fidelity; increased weekly mileage to 25, increased length of long runs to 10 miles, and integrated hills into training	Completed the half marathon

Of course, it is possible to demonstrate high fidelity but not achieve the desired outcome. Perhaps one of the runners followed the plan closely but twisted her ankle during the race and needed to drop out: high fidelity, poor outcome. It is also possible that the intervention, while implemented with high fidelity, was not effective for the situation. For example, these runners adapted a half marathon training plan in order to run in mountainous terrain. It is possible that their adaptations—even if adherence had been perfect—were not effective for the race they wanted to run.

Implementation fidelity is only one piece of the effective intervention puzzle. Because it is often overlooked in higher education research, we have included it here as a guide for conceptualizing and measuring implementation fidelity in learning improvement initiatives.

What Is Implementation Fidelity?

For decades, researchers in diverse disciplines have acknowledged the importance of studying the degree to which intended study conditions aligned with enacted conditions. Each discipline conceptualizes fidelity differently, prioritizing the measurement of different components of the treatment process (Zvoch, 2012). A variety of names are used to refer to a similar cluster of topics: *Intervention fidelity, treatment integrity, adherence, compliance, dose, exposure, quality of delivery,* and *treatment differentiation* are each used in different fields to discuss the concordance between actual and intended interventions (Hulleman & Cordray, 2009). This variation in the literature need not be a source of confusion; instead, we will provide a brief overview of perspectives on fidelity from different fields in order to encourage flexible application of these concepts. Different interventions may require different conceptualizations of fidelity, so it is useful to have a variety of models from which to draw guidance.

In medical research, "intervention fidelity" is considered important for replication of research as well as evaluation of study quality (Connelly, 2019): Understanding the degree to which the intervention was purely administered (with no omissions or additions) is crucial to interpretation of the study's findings (Toomey & Hardeman, 2017). Additionally, the process of ensuring intervention fidelity is expected to clarify the differences between the intervention under study and alternative interventions (Connelly, 2019). Murphy and Gutman (2012) provide guidance for designing high-fidelity medical trials. They list five strategies for increasing intervention fidelity: planning for setbacks (e.g., medical provider dropout during data collection); providing consistent, high-quality professional development for intervention providers;

developing written intervention manuals; documenting participants' compliance with the intervention; and measuring participants' application of the intervention contents in their lives. So important is this concept to medical research that entire journals have been devoted to its study (e.g., *Journal of Compliance in Health Care*, which was published for 4 years in the 1980s; Shadish et al., 2002).

The concept also appears regularly in program evaluation literature (under the terms *treatment fidelity* and *strength of treatment*; Mertens & Wilson, 2012). Treatment fidelity refers to the implementation of the program as intended, while strength of treatment refers to the match between the intended and actual *degree* of implementation. The central concept remains the same: Effective evaluation of an intervention requires us to know something about the degree to which the intervention actually occurred. Attention to the correspondence between the planned and delivered intervention within program evaluation can be traced to the 1970s, when evaluators, methodologists, and policy analysts realized that research not accounting for these factors could result in erroneous inferences about program efficacy (Zvoch, 2012).

Methodological texts, like Shadish et al.'s (2002) seminal book *Experimental and Quasi-Experimental Designs for Generalized Causal Inference*, also stress the importance of a critical eye for implementation quality. They describe three elements of implementation: treatment delivery (whether the treatment has been provided to the participant), treatment receipt (whether the participant receives the treatment), and treatment adherence (whether the participant participates fully in the intervention). These three components may overlap (as when a treatment is a surgical procedure, and the delivery and receipt of the treatment are one and the same; Shadish et al., 2002; Zvoch, 2012). Shadish et al. (2002) argue that implementation must be studied whenever research is conducted in real-world contexts, as deviations from the planned intervention are almost inevitable. Planning for these deviations and preparing systems for their detection and study is necessary to

> ensure that the intervention was actually manipulated, to detect and remedy problems with the interventions before they progress too far, to describe the nature of the intervention, to explore not just whether the intervention works but how it works, and to examine covariation between intervention and outcome. (Shadish et al., 2002, p. 316)

In other words, they argue that we should plan for our interventions to be implemented imperfectly. Implementation fidelity is the tool we use to monitor those imperfections.

Integration With Outcomes Assessment

Of course, implementation fidelity is not a substitute for the measurement of outcomes. Instead, we argue that both outcomes data and fidelity data are necessary in order to evaluate the quality of interventions. This idea has been extensively discussed by Sara Finney and colleagues (e.g., Finney & Smith, 2016, Fisher et al., 2014; Smith et al., 2019; Swain et al., 2013). To briefly summarize this work, implementation fidelity data is useful in determining whether our outcomes can be interpreted in the context of the *planned* intervention. Without information about the alignment of the planned and actual versions of the program, we cannot be sure which version of the intervention is reflected by the outcomes data. If implementation fidelity is poor, the outcomes do not necessarily reflect those that would have occurred if the program was implemented with high fidelity.

As a simplified example, consider the conclusions that can be drawn using four possible combinations of outcome data (the intended outcome was either achieved or not achieved) and fidelity data (high implementation fidelity or low implementation fidelity; Swain et al., 2013). First, consider two cases in which the intended outcomes of a program are not achieved. If the program is implemented with low fidelity and the intended outcomes are not achieved, nothing can be inferred about the effectiveness of the planned program. Because implementation fidelity is low, the program did not occur as planned, and no inferences can be made about its effectiveness. However, if the program is implemented with high fidelity and the intended outcomes are still not achieved, it can be inferred that the intended program was not effective for achieving the intended outcomes. In other words, if we know that the program was delivered as intended, we can more readily assume that the outcomes reflect the impact of the program *as it was planned*. This is not an assumption we can make in situations with low implementation fidelity.

What happens if assessment results show that the intended results have been achieved? If the program is implemented with low fidelity and outcomes data indicate that the intended outcomes have been achieved, then something other than the planned program is resulting in the observed outcomes. For example, it is possible that the implemented program was effective, even though it did not align with the planned program. It is also possible that something else in the learning environment outside of the intervention led to the intended results. Finally, if the program is implemented with high fidelity and the intended outcomes are achieved, the inference can be made that the planned program is effective. This situation—high fidelity and achievement of intended outcomes—is the ideal scenario when combining implementation fidelity data with assessment data.

Each of these combinations of outcome data and fidelity data points to different next steps. If the intended outcomes have not been achieved and fidelity is low, the program may be worth implementing again with a focus on increasing fidelity. If intended outcomes have not been achieved and fidelity is high, the next steps will likely entail a reexamination of the theory underlying the program, followed by adjustments to the intervention that are expected to fix the previous version's shortcomings. If the intended outcomes are met but fidelity is low, the next steps are somewhat more confusing: The program may not be necessary, or deviations from the intended program may represent a truly effective program. Further examination is necessary to determine which of these alternatives is most plausible. Finally, if the intended outcomes are met and fidelity is high, the next steps may include scaling up the program or expanding the intervention to serve additional outcomes.

Of course, a variety of validity issues must be examined when attempting to make causal claims about programs; the scope of this chapter does not permit a full examination of this topic. The interested reader may consider consulting Shadish et al. (2002) for more detailed information about causal claims in nonexperimental research.

Measuring Implementation Fidelity

Much like the varied names for implementation fidelity and similar concepts, several frameworks also exist for evaluating the strength of implementation fidelity. The interested reader may reference Dhillon et al. (2015) for an overview of conceptualizations of implementation fidelity. Here, we will use a five-part method first outlined by Dane and Schneider (1998). These five components—adherence, exposure, quality of delivery, participant responsiveness, and program differentiation—provide information about the structure of the intended program, the quality with which it is delivered, and the interaction between participants and the program itself.

Swain et al. (2013) demonstrated how these five elements can be used to develop checklists, which can then be used to record degrees of implementation fidelity. The implementation fidelity checklist contains information about the major components of the program, the SLOs the program is intended to address, and the specific features—such as activities, presentations, and assignments—that comprise the components. Prior to the implementation of the program, each of these elements should be clearly outlined, along with the amount of time that is to be devoted to each of the major components. This process, which is called program differentiation, might seem familiar. These are the same general steps taken while mapping the interventions to the SLOs. Here, we are organizing this information and specifying time allocations in order to structure program observations.

When the program is implemented, four more elements can be recorded: adherence, actual exposure, quality of delivery, and participant responsiveness. *Adherence*, which is typically documented as a simple "yes" or "no," indicates whether the identified program feature actually occurred. If so, the remaining three new elements can be evaluated. If not, they remain blank. *Actual exposure* provides the observational counterpart to the intended amount of time outlined during program differentiation. For this part of the checklist, the amount of time devoted to the component is recorded. *Quality of delivery* reflects the degree to which the feature was delivered well: Was the facilitator engaging and well prepared? Did the facilitator deliver content clearly? Finally, *responsiveness* reflects the degree to which the participants were engaged with or paying attention to the program. This, of course, looks different depending on the type of program. Responsiveness during a lecture manifests differently than responsiveness during a peer-review activity. Generally, the purpose here is to record the way that participants interact with the program feature. This is similar to the concept of "treatment adherence" discussed by Shadish et al. (2002). Appendix C contains a sample implementation fidelity checklist for intervention A from Xela and Rusty's program.

Of course, the checklist is of little worth if it is not used. Who, then, should complete the checklist during the program's implementation? A variety of approaches have been outlined in the literature, each accompanied by its own strengths and weaknesses. Breitenstein et al. (2010) outlined several options, as well as their limitations. The person administering the intervention (perhaps a course instructor) may complete the checklist. This person is (hopefully) familiar enough with the program that only minimal professional development is necessary to complete the checklist, and because that person is already present in the intervention, no additional person hours are necessary. However, biases such as social desirability may lead to inaccurately positive-quality reports. Additionally, facilitators may struggle to recall details (e.g., actual exposure time for each program component) if they are tasked with both implementing the intervention and evaluating its quality.

Another option is to use an independent observer. The observer may be physically present during the intervention, or a video or audio recording may be made for the observer to review later. Scheduling difficulties may diminish the feasibility of in-person observers, but audio and video recordings are now quite easy and cheap to create. While these approaches circumvent some of the issues identified with self-report, they are more resource intensive to implement. Particularly for long interventions (e.g., those that take place during multiple class meetings over the course of a semester), dozens of hours of observation (or of replaying recorded observations) may be required. Audio and video recording are also susceptible to technical difficulties and limited scope, as a single recording device is unlikely capable of capturing all the details of the program's implementation. An additional issue with any of the observation strategies is the possibility of behavioral changes due to knowledge of observation. Many of us would strive to perform at our best if we knew someone was watching or recording us. Although this could lead to increased implementation quality, it may instead lead to inflated estimates of implementation quality as observed sessions are implemented with higher fidelity than unobserved sessions.

Together, this means there is no single best way of completing an implementation fidelity checklist. The self-report and various observation-based methods each have strengths and limitations, and the best choice will rely on the qualities of the intervention and the resources available. If none of these methods are feasible, informal check-ins with intervention facilitators can also be used to gather some limited information about implementation. For example, time may be set aside during faculty meetings for brief discussions about instructors' experiences with the intervention. This method is far less time intensive than the other methods outlined, but it is also less likely to provide clear, actionable information than the other approaches.

Degrees of Implementation Fidelity

When designing a plan to measure implementation fidelity, a central consideration is the degree of uniformity with which the program is expected to be administered. Some program components, for example, might include detailed facilitation guides and scripts for presenters; others might be looser, such as when multiple facilitators are tasked with overseeing a flexible in-class activity. The development of the implementation fidelity checklist should reflect the degree to which facilitators are expected to move in tandem. Adherence to a common script, then, might be included in checklist criteria for strictly administered programs, while adherence to general guidelines for an activity might be more appropriate for inclusion in a checklist for more flexible programs. Fidelity and responsiveness to the needs of program recipients, therefore, are not necessarily incompatible (see Toomey & Hardeman 2017 for a discussion of this issue in the context of physical therapy).

As an example, consider three degrees of stringency in the implementation of an intervention in an introductory statistics course to improve students' skills in interpreting the results of a regression analysis. In the first intervention, five faculty members develop a lecture (including a script and a set of slides) and an in-class activity. All five facilitators are expected to deliver the lecture verbatim and provide the same directions and debriefing information for the activity. In this case, high fidelity would require the facilitators to be more or less interchangeable: Students in each section should have nearly identical experiences during the intervention. In the second intervention, each of the five faculty members is tasked with creating a lecture and activity targeting the outcome. The fidelity checklist contains general descriptions of the program components (e.g., a 30-minute lesson on interpreting regression results and a 20-minute activity) and basic guidelines for the activity. Each of the five facilitators therefore approaches the presentation and the activity in slightly different ways. In the third intervention, all facilitators are charged with addressing the SLO, but no further guidelines are provided. An implementation fidelity checklist cannot be developed when so much flexibility is offered.

It is easy to imagine the problems that may arise in the first scenario. It is likely that each of the five faculty members has different strengths, weaknesses, and preferred teaching styles, and it is therefore unlikely that the five could easily decide on a mutually agreeable scripted lecture and activity. Although this scenario lends itself well to the collection of detailed implementation fidelity information, it might not be a realistic approach for all instructor groups. In the third scenario, conceptualizing implementation fidelity is difficult, if not impossible. Although this approach provides the most flexibility to the faculty implementers, it does not lend itself well to collecting fidelity data. The second scenario is likely to be the most realistic in many academic situations: Enough structure is provided that implementation fidelity data can be collected, but each facilitator is provided with some degree of latitude in their delivery method. As always, the choice of stringency level is context dependent, and careful consideration is necessary when balancing the needs and desires of facilitators with the desire for similarity.

Even within a single program, different levels of stringency might be adopted. Recall Xela and Rusty's intervention plans, in which interventions were distributed across three courses. The faculty teams teaching two courses opted for highly prescriptive interventions. The third faculty team opted for a moderate level of stringency. For every team, the faculty were comfortable with delivering interventions at the agreed-on level of uniformity.

Concluding Thoughts

This chapter described how to monitor the process of transforming a learning improvement plan into action. The most critical step is helping faculty deliver the changed learning environment (i.e., the newly developed interventions) as intended. Of course, it is nearly inevitable that deviations will occur. This is precisely the point of collecting implementation fidelity data. Combining information about student outcomes *and* implementation fidelity puts improvement efforts in a more powerful place to evaluate the effectiveness of their interventions. The collection of implementation fidelity data is also likely to uncover important information about the feasibility and delivery of interventions that can be used to refine future versions of the program. Of course, delivering interventions with high fidelity is not easy. However, the likelihood of success can be increased by providing faculty with adequate support (and time) to integrate new assignments and processes into their classrooms.

The past five chapters have discussed the process of preparing for and implementing the major steps of a learning improvement intervention. The next chapter begins the process of stitching the information together to compare learning environments and student performance through the process of reassessment. Together, this information can be used to tell a powerful learning improvement story.

Exercises

1. Give an example from your own experience where you were asked to teach something new but were not well prepared to do it.

2. Give an example from your own experience where you were asked to teach something new and were given helpful support. How was this support designed?

3. Think about a program you are affiliated with and imagine you were attempting a learning improvement project.

    a. What courses will be affected?

    b. Who teaches those courses?

    c. Draw it out, using Figure 8.1 as a reference.

    d. Why is it imperative that *all* of those instructors are committed to the project?

4. What is implementation fidelity and why might it be helpful in the learning improvement context?

    a. Provide an example you have seen of extremely low implementation fidelity.

    b. Provide an example you have seen of moderate implementation fidelity.

    c. Provide an example you have seen of complete implementation fidelity.

5. Craft a short persuasive presentation about why your colleagues should consider implementation fidelity when evaluating the effectiveness of interventions.

9

REASSESSMENT

This chapter will detail the reassessment process, during which the level of student achievement is again measured and compared to baseline levels in order to determine whether learning has improved. This chapter will also discuss how to determine when sufficient progress has been made, as well as what to do when results are less than optimal.

Now we come to the last part of the simple model. It is the reassessment that indicates whether learning improvement occurred. We hope to be able to support the claim that the changes made to the learning environment (interventions) had the desired effect of improving student learning. If a team has carefully attended to the other components of learning improvement, the reassessment process is relatively straightforward. In essence, the same procedure used for collecting baseline data should be reapplied to the cohort of students who received the changed learning environment.

As with baseline data collection, two types of data should be captured: performance data (what do students know, or what are they able to do?) and environmental data (what is the educational context the students have experienced?). Investigating how the learning environment has affected student performance—before and after interventions—is at the crux of making a learning improvement claim. Returning to the bodybuilding example, we would need to examine physique (performance baseline) along with food intake, workout regimen, and general health (environmental baseline) before and after intervening in order to determine whether the intervention worked. Simply evaluating physique before and after the intervention does not generate sufficient evidence to claim that the intervention has resulted in improvement. We must also understand what (if anything) in the environment changed between the two time points if we want to attribute changes in physique to changes in the environment.

Let's go back to Rusty and Xela's example. They measured student ability using three instruments in 4 consecutive years. Students' baseline performance in year 1 was poor for all three measures (see the first row of Table 9.1).

TABLE 9.1
Assessment Results and Intervention Implementation, Years 1 and 4

Time	Results
Year 1	Multiple choice (SLO 1): 12.5/30 Short answer (SLO 2): 5.6/15 Embedded assessment (SLO 3): 4.2/15 Jessica 201.01 201.02 - Xela 201.03 201.04 - Gabe 201.05 201.06 - Yelisey 201.07 201.08 - Rebecca 201.09 201.10 - Kurt 310.01 310.02 - Shaun 310.03 310.04 - Kevin 310.05 310.06 - Ali 310.07 310.08 C Gus 310.09 310.10 - Katherine 495.01 495.02 495.03 - Rusty 495.04 495.05 495.06 - Andrea 495.07 495.08 495.09 - Daigo 495.10 495.11 495.12 - Theresa 495.13 495.14 495.15 -
Year 4	Multiple choice (SLO 1): 24.0/30 Short answer (SLO 2): 13.1/15 Embedded assessment (SLO 3): 12.9/15 Jessica 201.01 201.02 A B Xela 201.03 201.04 B Gabe 201.05 201.06 A B Yelisey 201.07 201.08 A B Rebecca 201.09 201.10 A B Kurt 310.01 310.02 C Shaun 310.03 310.04 C D Kevin 310.05 310.06 C D Ali 310.07 310.08 C D Gus 310.09 310.10 C D Katherine 495.01 495.02 495.03 E F G Rusty 495.04 495.05 495.06 E G Andrea 495.07 495.08 495.09 E F G Daigo 495.10 495.11 495.12 E F Theresa 495.13 495.14 495.15 E F G

Recall that only one faculty member, Ali, had any course components related to context-aligned writing at the time of the baseline measurement. He had been implementing a brief version of what would later become intervention C. The top portion of Table 9.1 shows the performance baseline and the environmental baseline. Each faculty member is represented by a box, which is shaded in correspondence with that faculty member's effectiveness at teaching aligned writing. Highly effective instructors have black boxes, somewhat effective instructors are gray, while ineffective instructors are white. Notice that the box representing Ali's sections is gray while the other instructors' boxes are white. This indicates that Ali is more effective at teaching this particular skill than his colleagues. Note, too, the letter "C" in his box. This represents the (early form of) intervention C being implemented in his sections at the time of the baseline measurement. The dash present in the other instructors' boxes reflects the absence of interventions on aligned writing being implemented in the other sections at the time of baseline measurement. Each box also lists the course and sections each instructor teaches. For example, Katherine teaches sections 1, 2, and 3 of PSYC 495.

Now examine the bottom portion of Table 9.1. Several changes are evident. First, most instructors are implementing the planned interventions in their courses. (as indicated by the capital letters at the bottom of each box). Additionally, the shading of each instructors' box has darkened. This indicates that every single instructor has become more effective at teaching students how to align their writing to a given context or task. Although not all instructors are highly effective, none of them are completely ineffective at teaching this content any longer.

In these new circumstances, how could learning not improve? The program started with virtually no coverage of contextually aligned writing in any of their courses. In the next 3 years, faculty were provided with opportunities to develop their skills and their course designs. They implemented dozens of hours of evidence-informed interventions across three courses. They developed assessments closely aligned with the other components of the learning system, leading to an exceptionally strong improvement "signal" with minimal methodological noise. In contrast, in our many observations of less successful improvement efforts, the intervention signal is typically weak, and the methodology is noisy. Undoubtedly, this contributes to our national paucity of learning improvement examples.

Nevertheless, Rusty and Xela's example is almost too good. In fact, we anticipate when institutions first engage in improving student learning at scale, their results will not be as robust nor their processes as smooth. As elaborated in chapter 3, learning improvement at scale can be thwarted by any fundamental flaw or an accumulation of small missteps.

We cannot stress enough that it is okay if a learning improvement effort falls short. In these cases, how institutions, faculty, and administrators respond is of tantamount importance. Do they make the same mistakes in their next learning improvement effort (or, worse, abandon future efforts entirely)? Or do they become smarter, enhance their process for supporting and implementing improvement efforts, and work toward creating a higher probability of success for each subsequent initiative?

We provide alternate realities for Rusty and Xela's program. In each, the program endeavors to improve student writing but the improvement initiatives vary regarding their effectiveness. Nevertheless, the program responds proactively to each of these progressively more mature learning improvement efforts. In no scenario do they deny reality or lack the will to improve. You can imagine them reflecting on their initiative after reading this book. Every scenario is beneficial in the sense that they are building on past mistakes and capitalizing on their existing strengths.

Scenario 1: Fundamental Flaws

Three years ago, prompted by a department meeting, several faculty members committed to devoting more time to student writing. Two attended how-to-teach-writing workshops facilitated a by the university. Occasionally, a few faculty members would meet to talk about their individual efforts in their own sections. They recently collected assessment data from their seniors using a rubric they found online. Some faculty members submitted student writing samples, but many others did not.

The department met to reflect on the project. The faculty agreed that they had learned much in the past 3 years, and a few individual faculty members made claims that they believed students in their course sections were better writers than students a few years ago.

Nevertheless, as a learning improvement at-scale project, it lacked fundamental components and integration. It was as if construction workers began building a house with no architectural blueprint. Cement was poured onto the ground, some wires were thrown into the mix, and shingles were laid about. In some cases, the quality of materials was good, and in some places the process of applying those materials was smooth. Nevertheless, the materials and processes had not been coordinated to build a coherent structure.

In retrospect, the faculty members realized they were missing significant chunks of necessary information. They had not spent enough time defining their learning area, selecting an instrument, thinking about where interventions might be implemented to reach all students, considering the efficacy of particular interventions, developing faculty's professional skills in teaching writing, creating plans for high-quality and consistent assessment before and after the intervention, and so forth.

On the positive side, the group was critically reflecting on learning from a program's perspective. Up to this point, most of the departmental faculty reflected critically about their own classes and had made adjustments at that level. Now, they were scaling up their self-reflection, thinking about their team of faculty, the overall goals for student learning, and what they needed to do to be more successful as a unit. Further, there was much to build on.

They realized that their colleagues care about student learning. They also found that the department's faculty members would sacrifice some of their independence if it meant that students had a shot at becoming better writers. Furthermore, the department head was open to listening to more strategic ways to improve learning. In other words, the program may be ready for another improvement initiative. The next time, they will move forward with their eyes wide open.

Scenario 2: Good Learning System, not Implemented at Scale

Xela spots the issues with her students' writing and gets to work. She identifies contextually aligned writing as the construct she would like to improve and builds several exercises in her courses around it. She finds that her students' writing gets better over a few cohorts. On the positive side, Xela has designed and implemented a learning system effectively. The bad news is that Xela only teaches a small fraction of the students. This is not an example of learning improvement at scale. Nevertheless, she has built much on which to expand.

Imagine if Xela were a junior faculty member. This might be a golden opportunity for a department head to ask Xela if she would be interested in working with other faculty members to expand the improvement effort. In this case, Xela needs to build a collective will to improve, and then work with her colleagues to scale up the initiative.

Scenario 3: Implementation Woes

In this scenario, the program has succeeded on the front-end work. The faculty are all on board to improve contextually aligned writing. The vision is laid out, the assessment instruments well designed, and the interventions well researched. However, when the reassessment comes around, the gain from cohort to cohort is much smaller than anticipated. What happened? Xela and her colleagues investigated and realized that the best-laid plans had not been implemented as intended. Because of a last-minute conflict, 10 of the 15 faculty were unable to participate in a 3-day summer implementation workshop, the space designed to help faculty think through and build out interventions with their individual classes. Indeed, the 10 nonattendees revealed they implemented the interventions only minimally. Fortunately, because the program did an adequate job of collecting performance and environmental data, the process breakdown was relatively easy to troubleshoot. The team could offer the 3-day workshop again at a time available to the remaining faculty members.

These three scenarios are a mere sample of the myriad ways learning improvement initiatives fall short of their potential. And again, there is no shame in being imperfect, especially if the individuals involved learn from the situation. But what happens when the system works?

What Happens Next?

When a legitimate example of learning improvement at scale is accomplished, it should not be kept a secret. It's a feat worth sharing and celebrating. In Xela and Rusty's example, they presented at conferences with other faculty and with students. The provost asked the inner circle of the learning improvement team to share their story with the senior leadership of the academic division. The university's president made it a point to congratulate the team during the university's yearly presidential address. In other words, the faculty and administrators realized how difficult and important this victory was.

Over time, victories such as Xela and Rusty's should become more common and less difficult because the learning improvement mindset and skills are contagious. Once one program figures out how to work together to produce learning improvement, other early adopters will follow. Within a few years, administrators, faculty, and staff will hopefully begin to work collectively on learning improvement at-scale projects as a matter of habit. The next two chapters (10 and 11) show how this learning evolution could happen.

Learning Improvement: A Summary

Our goal for this book has been to lay the foundation for how higher education can organize efforts to promote learning improvement. While the details described in each chapter are meaningful, we argue that it is the over-all heuristic that is most important. We briefly summarize, for the final time, the most salient points in the learning improvement process:

- Build a coalition of faculty who are ready and willing to support a learning improvement effort.
- Create a clear vision of what the program hopes that a student can know, think, or do as a function of the learning improvement effort, including articulation of the vision through selection or development of an assessment tool.
- Gain a full understanding of the current learning system relative to the targeted SLO by collecting baseline data on student performance and on the learning environment itself.
- Determine what changes to the learning environment would likely improve the targeted SLO.
- Provide the faculty implementers with professional development so they are prepared to implement the interventions with fidelity.
- Reassess the SLO data and the learning-environment data to ascertain whether the learning improvement effort was successful.
- Celebrate and take advantage of what has been learned to embark on other learning improvement efforts.

Throughout this book, we have used a fictional academic degree program as an example of successful learning improvement at scale. Nevertheless, most of the principles and strategies outlined in this book could be adapted for student affairs programs (see Appendix A for a brief example). Additionally, we believe many of the strategies could be further extrapolated to broader institutional effectiveness areas, such as retention. In the years to come, we hope to see—and participate in—applications of learning improvement strategies in new realms and disciplines.

Learning Improvement as a Higher Education Strategy

Chapters 4 through 9 laid out the strategy for improving student learning at scale within a *single* academic degree program at a *single* institution. We believe improvement at this scale is the building block for broader improvement efforts at higher levels. The next and final section of this book focuses on improvement at the institutional and national levels.

Exercises

1. Why is reassessment necessary for improvement efforts?
2. Why does knowing the educational environment data at the time of reassessment help with the interpretation of assessment data?
3. What is implementation fidelity data? Why is it helpful to interpret implementation fidelity data in tandem with assessment data?
4. If a program you were affiliated with demonstrated learning improvement at scale, what steps would you take next?

PART THREE

EXPANDING LEARNING IMPROVEMENT AT SCALE

10

DOING HIGHER EDUCATION AS IF LEARNING IMPROVEMENT MATTERS MOST

In this chapter, we pay homage to Thomas Angelo's (1999) classic paper "Doing Assessment as if Learning Matters Most," submitted more than 2 decades ago to the American Association of Higher Education. Like Angelo, we endeavor to paint an aspirational picture of the future of higher education and outline strategies to make this future state a reality. First, we note our reasons for the title of this chapter. Second, we provide a vision of what higher education could look like in 20 years. Third, we lay out five developmental stages for learning improvement in higher education. Fourth, we identify key strategies to ascend through the developmental stages. And last, we remind everyone why higher education must go this direction.

B y the late 1990s, higher education's push for learning assessment was about 20 years old. The concept of formalized program-level assessment was therefore relatively new, but it had been around long enough for scholars to begin to reflect on what worked and what did not. Thomas Angelo was already considered one of higher education assessment's pioneers. He and K. Patricia Cross (Angelo & Cross, 1993) had published the popular and influential text *Classroom Assessment Techniques: A Handbook for College Teachers* just a few years earlier. In other words, Angelo was at the time (and continues to be) one of the most influential scholars in higher education.

It was during this time that Angelo (1999) published "Doing Assessment as if Learning Matters Most." In this article, Angelo argued that transformation in higher education would only be possible in the context of a compelling vision of the future, new conceptual models of assessment, and empirically informed guidelines for quality practice. In Angelo's imagined future, assessment is presented as the vehicle for achieving learning improvement in higher

139

education, but only if we can shake ourselves loose of add-on and episodic assessment paradigms. He noted that assessment is often treated as an end unto itself, where merely conducting assessment is the goal. Instead, he argued that learning improvement should be the end goal, and that assessment should serve as the means to achieve that goal. Now, 40 years after the beginning of the assessment movement and more than 20 years after Angelo shared his vision, it is again time to think about assessment and improvement more carefully.

Similar Titles, an Important Distinction

We agree with the spirit of Angelo's argument: Assessment should not be treated as an end unto itself. Instead, the rightful emphasis should be placed on improving student learning. We also believe that many of his suggested strategies in 1999 are just as relevant as today. For example, Angelo suggested that institutions should lower barriers to change and that academics should collaborate on shared goals related to learning.

Nevertheless, Angelo's article highlighted assessment as a key means to improve student learning. We disagree with this framing. As we and others before us (e.g., Brown & Knight, 1994) have pointed out, a pig never fattened because it was weighed. With respect to learning improvement, assessment is neither an end nor a critical means to a more virtuous end. Centralizing assessment overemphasizes the role of assessment in learning improvement efforts. Instead, we believe it is higher education as a whole that must be better integrated and more thoughtfully designed in order to catalyze learning improvement. Although assessment must play an important role in this revolution, it should not take the titular role. Notice that *assessment* is not even in the title of this chapter.

We present an updated vision for the future of higher education. Instead of focusing on the role of *assessment* in higher education, though, we focus on the role of a larger system of *learning improvement*. Our revised vision requires academe to think more strategically about the role of education systems in achieving learning improvement. How do we achieve better SLOs, at scale, by integrating the constituent pieces of higher education into effective learning systems?

Vision 2041: Learning Improvement Prevalence

Chapter 5 discussed how a clearly articulated vision of student learning improvement guides learning improvement initiatives. Now, we return to the importance of vision, this time with a much wider scope. What could colleges and universities look like 20 years from now if we approached higher education as if learning improvement mattered most? Here is our aspiration. By 2041, we envision that

- every college in the United States will have demonstrated at least one successful example of institutional-level learning improvement (e.g., improvement in some knowledge or skill area that affects all undergraduates) during the previous decade, and
- within each institution, every academic program will show at least one successful example—ideally, multiple examples—of learning improvement in the same time period. For instance, if an institution offers 100 academic degree and certificate programs, each of those programs will show one example of learning improvement.

Achieving this vision would mean thousands of U.S. institutional-level learning improvement examples and tens (maybe hundreds) of thousands of program-level improvement examples. Recall that today, across the United States' entire higher education system, we only have a handful of examples at either level. What would it take to go from today's virtual absence of learning improvement to learning improvement prevalence in 2041?

The path is not easy. In fact, the distance between where we are now and this vision for 2041 is so great that it may seem insurmountable. However, broken down into smaller pieces, this large task becomes more manageable.

Developmental Stages to Improvement

The path to learning improvement prevalence will not happen overnight, or even within the span of a few years. Each institution will need to pass through a series of developmental stages in which their capacity, skills, and resources to support learning improvement slowly increase in sophistication and coordination. The successive stages are described in the following sections.

Clueless

The first stage is not a good one. The institution at this level pays little attention to learning, let alone learning improvement. Such schools often make dramatic claims about what students will gain from the institutional experiences that they offer, but the claims are largely (or entirely) unfounded. Faculty rarely talk about learning with each other and they lack access to professional development. If the institution conducts learning outcomes assessment at all, the goal is to form a smoke screen to deter accreditors' scrutiny.

If the institution has curriculum maps, they bear little resemblance to reality. Fortunately, from our view, most institutions are beyond this level.

Good Intentions

If we had to estimate the status of most colleges in the United States, this would be our best guess. The institution and the people who work within it care about learning. Many faculty members participate in pedagogically oriented professional development. Assessment is conducted at the program level. Faculty regularly make changes to programs with the intention of generating improvements. The shortcoming, though, is that changes are made in disconnected silos. Program-level learning improvement is not evidenced because faculty, administrators, institutions, and accreditors do not work in tandem to achieve improvement goals. In essence, frequent individual attempts to improve student learning fail to result in program-level improvement because no structure exists to coordinate well-intended efforts.

Improvement Threshold

The third level is an important one. This type of institution can demonstrate one legitimate example of program-level learning improvement. This success signifies that, at least in some departments, the institution has the will, skill, and coordination to execute learning improvement. We believe the tools contained in this book will help institutions achieve this level. This step is a launching point to a better paradigm for higher education because it provides a local proof of concept for the promises of learning improvement.

Improvement Incubator

At this level, the institution elicits, supports, and promotes successful learning improvement. The school has a formal mechanism for selecting and supporting program-level (and perhaps institution-level) learning improvement initiatives. Many faculty and staff have moderate knowledge and skills about learning improvement at scale (commensurate with those who have read this book and have attempted a learning improvement at-scale project). Furthermore, the institution employs a handful of professionals with experience and success facilitating and supporting learning improvement efforts. For example, faculty developers and assessment professionals have a history of collaboration and mutual facilitation of improvement initiatives. People in senior leadership positions understand that one of their most important duties is to support the success of learning systems. They hire faculty and staff based not only on their expertise in assessment and/or faculty development, but also their ability to facilitate learning improvement efforts. The institution has a record of allocating funds in support of improvement endeavors. For example, money is set aside for teams of faculty members to work together in the summer to work on learning improvement projects. Successful learning improvement initiatives are visibly celebrated. A few universities (including our own) are on the cusp of achieving this level.

Improvement Prevalence

At this stage, learning improvement is no longer considered a rare achievement. Instead, it is seen as a core component of institutional culture. Contributions to learning improvement teams are considered favorably during faculty review processes, on a similar level to a publication in a top-tier journal. New faculty receive professional development on what it means to be part of an educational team, and how to understand their program as a coordinated, intentional learning system. Administrators are hired, in part, based on their past success of effectively supporting learning improvement efforts or their ability to propose specific plans for future efforts.

Improvement prevalence at an institution does not require that every person tries to improve everything simultaneously. For example, the prospect of an academic degree program improving all its SLOs each year is ludicrous. Instead, faculty in these institutions select relatively few outcomes to improve but commit resources to conducting each effort rigorously. This context creates an environment in which every program demonstrates an example of learning improvement on an SLO each decade. Similarly, an institution-level SLO—one that affects all undergraduates—is improved each decade.

Up to this point, we have been describing these developmental levels from the institutional perspective. This is because the institutions and the programs within them are where improvement happens. However, achieving the 2041 vision requires infrastructure not only within institutions but also around them. The next two sections describe how professional development and accreditation, respectively, could evolve to better support learning improvement. Importantly, these steps require action from individual faculty members up to the boards of accrediting bodies; fortunately, this means that there are ample opportunities at all levels of the higher education system for fostering a new culture of learning improvement.

Strategy 1: Professional Development

Progression through the developmental stages requires extensive knowledge and skill. Individuals need not only be adept in curricular design, pedagogy, project management, and measurement, but also in their integration. Professional development must therefore be offered by catering to multiple levels of experience and skill. We imagine four levels of sophistication, outlined next, to be targeted by professional development offerings. As a reminder, the responsibility for achieving these levels of sophistication falls jointly on the learning improvement leader-to-be as well as their institution's administration. While it is up to the individual leaders in training to seek out and engage in the opportunities outlined here, administrators are responsible for creating the conditions that allow such cross-training to occur.

Prerequisites

Learning improvement requires higher educators to think about and integrate different facets of educational systems. Therefore, to be in a position to take professional development related to learning improvement, we suggest that higher education professionals cross-train (Pope & Fulcher, 2019). In other words, these people will ideally have experience in teaching, faculty development, and assessment. To this point, recent articles have called for a deeper collaboration among assessment professionals, faculty developers, and instructors in support of student learning improvement (Kinzie et al., 2019; Reder & Crimmins, 2018). Here, we briefly describe three opportunities for cross-training.

1. Teach a college course. Without having experience inside a classroom, it will be very difficult to conceptualize how the pieces fit together. Faculty members will almost certainly have experience teaching courses, but faculty developers and assessment professionals might not. Reder and Crimmins (2018) argue that assessment professionals and faculty developers who have little experience teaching may not be able to adequately empathize with the real-world constraints of the college classroom.
2. Complete a course redesign workshop. These 3- to 5-day workshops help faculty reflect on their teaching and align SLOs, curriculum, pedagogy, and assessment at the section level. Even for people whose job responsibilities do not include teaching, participating in a course redesign workshop (perhaps through an observation role) is crucial in order to gain an inside view of the process.
3. Complete a workshop on program-level assessment. These workshops build assessment knowledge and reframe assessment as a program-level endeavor. They often cover basic methodological and logistical considerations in conducting program-level assessment. Ideally, this experience would be coupled with serving as an assessment coordinator for a program.

Professional development across these areas is key because it is impossible for even the most well-meaning people to integrate knowledge and experiences they do not have. Other useful tools for expanding knowledge and experience are the wide variety of webinars, workshops, books, certificate programs, and even doctoral programs in student learning outcomes assessment, faculty development, and effective pedagogy.

In contrast to the abundant resources on teaching, faculty development, and assessment, there are exceptionally few resources available on learning improvement at scale. Smith et al. (2015) found that most assessment books allude to improvement but provide few details about how to achieve it (beyond extolling the virtues of "closing the loop"). Faculty development books are typically designed to help one faculty member work on one class (Condon et al. (2016) being a notable exception). Moving outside the sphere of typical higher education learning literature, one can start to find resources related to practical matters of improvement. For example, the Carnegie Foundation for the Advancement of Teaching (n.d.) has focused on improvement science. One of our favorite resources from this group—*Learning to Improve: How America's Schools Can Get Better at Getting Better* (Bryk et al., 2017)—provides practical guidance for conceptualizing and implementing improvement strategies. Nevertheless, it focuses mainly on elementary and secondary education and provides only brief treatment of the improvement of SLOs specifically.

Professional development opportunities can evolve to prepare faculty to improve student learning at scale in higher education. We envision professional development targeted at various levels of sophistication. Next, we describe three levels of sophistication, their goals, and the types of professional development they might entail.

Introductory Professional Development

For learning improvement at scale to take hold, most higher education professionals need to know what learning improvement is. This level of professional development, then, serves to build conceptual awareness. One of the current problems in higher education is that many faculty and staff erroneously believe they have witnessed or participated in examples of improvement at scale. As we have discussed extensively, proper scrutiny frequently reveals these "improvements" merely to be "changes," and it is often unclear how many students they affect. Introductory professional development should include a basic overview of the necessary resources and conditions for evidencing learning improvement at the intended scale. In our experience, a half-day workshop is appropriate for achieving these aims.

Fulcher et al.'s (2014) article introducing the concept of learning improvement can also serve this role.

Intermediate Professional Development

At this level, the goal is to prepare individuals to participate in a learning improvement at-scale initiative. This book has been designed to fulfill this need. Chapters 4 through 9 lay out the steps, and the exercises at the end of each chapter provide opportunities to practice relevant concepts. We hope that readers of this book feel confident enough to attempt a learning improvement at-scale endeavor of their own, hopefully with a group of similarly prepared colleagues. We could also foresee multiday workshops serving the same purpose and complementing the concepts discussed in this book.

Advanced Professional Development

If learning improvement at scale is one of the most important goals of higher education, it makes sense to professionalize the endeavor. Furthermore, to achieve our vision for 2041, higher education needs leaders who can oversee, coordinate, and enable learning improvement endeavors within their respective institutions. In fact, we could envision a world where professional development and assessment offices are subsumed under a larger learning improvement office.

At least two pathways can lead to professionalization in learning improvement. The first focuses on helping professionals in complementary fields (e.g., assessment and faculty development) transform into learning improvement professionals. This approach would provide cross-training, as outlined previously, integrated with a strong foundation of relevant existing skills. Individuals pursuing this path would have experiences planning and overseeing several learning improvement endeavors. Perhaps a certificate program could help formalize their existing skills into formal professional recognition.

The second pathway is to create a graduate program focusing on learning improvement at scale. Students might take courses in learning theory, assessment, measurement, facilitation, and change management. Furthermore, through the course of the program, students would be given progressively greater responsibility in ongoing learning improvement projects. For example, at the beginning of the program, they may read case studies about learning improvement and provide feedback. In the middle of the program, they may be the "understudy" of the champion on a learning improvement project. By the end of the program—perhaps as a capstone project—they should have experience acting as a project's cochampion.

Table 10.1 summarizes professional development opportunities for different levels of improvement skills.

While a handful of people around the country are giving introductory workshops on learning improvement at scale (or something close to it), they are not widespread. We envision a sharp rise in such workshops, which may be affiliated with regional accreditors, assessment conferences, or faculty development and SoTL conferences.

Nevertheless, we believe that preparing most people to be part of learning improvement teams will require more than an introductory workshop.

TABLE 10.1
Professional Development Across Levels of Learning Improvement Skill

Desired Level	Goal	Types of Professional Development and Relevant Experiences
Prerequisite	Building foundational knowledge	• Teach a college course • Attend multiday assessment workshop and/or serve as a program assessment coordinator • Attend multiday course redesign workshop
Introductory	Developing awareness of the learning improvement model	• Complete an introductory workshop on learning improvement • Read and discuss Fulcher et al. (2014)
Intermediate	Developing the ability to contribute to the learning improvement at-scale team	• Read and complete exercises contained in this book • Complete a multiday workshop on learning improvement
Professional	Building leaders capable of overseeing and coordinating learning improvement efforts	• Professional faculty developers or assessment experts take advantage of intermediate resources *and* successfully implement several learning improvement projects • Complete yet-to-be-developed graduate program in learning improvement

We envision organizations and institutions, perhaps in partnership with educational foundations, offering multiday workshops. These are the types of intensive professional development opportunities that will enable educators to enact learning improvement efforts on their own campuses. Furthermore, we could imagine more and more existing assessment and faculty development conferences adopting a learning improvement track. There, attendees can focus on the whole of learning improvement as opposed to the mere components. (A nod of appreciation is owed to Indiana University Purdue University Indianapolis' Assessment Institute for being an early adopter; their learning improvement track was added to the conference in 2018.)

Finally, for the highest levels of professional development, the movement will need universities who are willing to create learning improvement doctoral programs or concentrations within existing doctoral programs. Graduates from such programs can guide this new field by conducting research, integrating relevant strategies from higher education and beyond, and providing professional development to others.

Strategy 2: Policy/Accreditation

This second strategy will be considered more controversial given that higher education scholars such as Trudy Banta (2007) and Peter Ewell (2009) have opined about the strained relationship between accountability and improvement. But if we as educators truly value improvement and believe that it should be part of our fabric, then we will need assistance from the powerful entities associated with accountability. For example, each regional accreditor could develop a standard related to learning improvement. In perfect alignment with our vision for 2041, this may include a requirement that every school demonstrate one example of learning improvement at the institution level and one example for every academic degree and certificate program during each accreditation cycle.

The key here is for accreditors and, by extension, their review teams to meaningfully support learning improvement. As we mentioned earlier in the book, the spirit of accreditation is quality improvement. Unfortunately, evidence of improvement is lost somewhere between the intent of accreditors and what is submitted by institutions.

Let us be clear that we are not trying to throw accreditors under the bus. They are far from the only group with a checkered history relative to improvement. Assessment professionals too have been misrepresenting improvement and assessment's relationship to it (Smith et al., 2015). In fact, until about 2012, the first author (Fulcher) was part of this misinformation.

It wasn't because assessment professionals were purposefully misleading but because we did not clearly conceptualize learning improvement ourselves. So, why would we expect accreditors to put forth a more advanced view?

Regional and disciplinary accreditors could be excellent allies in the movement to improve student learning. For the next 10 years or so, they could work to encourage improvement efforts on campuses across the country. They could develop clear, rigorous standards against which to evaluate learning improvement efforts. Fulcher et al. (2017) provide an outline of how these new standards could be structured. The programs and institutions that meet the standards could be publicly commended and upheld as models. In 15 to 20 years, perhaps the momentum and capability could be strong enough to realistically expect a successful example of learning improvement at every college and university in the country.

Concluding Thoughts

Moving from the current state of affairs to what we envision for 2041 requires both bottom-up and top-down strategies. At the foundational level, higher education needs instructors cross-trained in teaching, faculty development, and assessment. In the middle, institutional administrators can provide the environment through which improvement can flourish. At the top, accreditors can help institutions stay focused on learning improvement by providing clear guidelines and feedback.

We will close this chapter by slightly modifying the words Angelo (1999) chose to conclude his own article: If we plan and conduct higher education at every step as if learning improvement matters most—not just the students' learning improvement, but ours, as well—then the distance between means and ends will be reduced and our chances of success increased.

JOIN THE IMPROVEMENT MOVEMENT: WHAT YOU CAN DO NOW

Throughout this book, we have provided detailed explanations for developing, implementing, and evaluating learning improvement at-scale initiatives. In this chapter we discuss steps that can be taken by anyone. They are particularly applicable if your institution or organization is in the early developmental stages of improvement.

The vision introduced in chapter 10—one in which higher education is built to encourage, support, and reinforce learning improvement at scale—is far from our current reality. So, what can you do right now? We have two broad recommendations that anyone who reads this book can start applying immediately. First, we advocate for speaking carefully and clearly about improvement. Second, we urge readers to initiate learning improvement at their own institution or organization. Changes in language and action are both necessary steps for revolutionizing the way improvement is approached in higher education.

Talk the Talk

A major obstacle to learning improvement is miscommunication. Higher educators use the word *improvement* when they really mean *change*. They confuse changes to the assessment process with changes to the learning environment (Fulcher & Prendergast, 2019). Some assessment professionals advocate for assessment as a pathway to learning improvement but are unaware of the importance of intentional changes to the learning environment.

Some campus leaders urge implementation of sweeping changes to a program or institution but have had no experience leading effective, coordinated change efforts. These misconceptions and overstatements collectively harm our ability to improve student learning in higher education.

Such miscommunication is even more detrimental when espoused by conference presenters, book authors, or writers of accreditation standards. The strategies endorsed by people with platforms in higher education influence how the field as a whole approaches problems, evidence, and change. If they relay the message that assessment solves all institutional ills, or that change can be achieved through individual and disconnected efforts, then those are the strategies that will be pursued. Holding ourselves and others to a higher standard of articulation is critical to refining the national conversation about educational improvement. We believe that strategically altering the way we discuss learning improvement in higher education will begin to change the way we approach improvement efforts as a discipline.

First, we suggest ensuring that the words *change* and *improvement* are used carefully and correctly. Throughout this book, we have defined *learning improvement* as documented increases in student proficiency that can reasonably be attributed to systematic changes in the learning environment. Further, we have differentiated program-level improvements—those changes that impact all students in a program—from improvements that occur in individual courses or course sections. To demonstrate program-level learning improvement, a program must gather baseline data about student proficiency, change the learning environment in a way that will impact all students, and reassess to determine student proficiency under the new learning environment. The comparison of the baseline data and the reassessment must show that students who experienced the changed learning environment perform better than students who did not. Simply put, if any of these components are missing, there is no evidence of learning improvement. Reserving the word *improvement* for examples in which these criteria are met draws a distinction between the changes that happen frequently on college campuses and the intentional, coordinated efforts we advocate for throughout this book. Other forms of change are important and worth celebrating, but they reflect a different type of strategy than a learning improvement effort. Improvement should never serve as a euphemism for change.

Second, we suggest changing the way we engage in conversations about improvement. When you hear people talk about improvement efforts, be inquisitive. The goal is not to "trap" a colleague using the language of improvement incorrectly, but to apply the same critical eye to these efforts that we apply to the rest of our work in higher education. Consider asking some of the following questions about their work:

- Which students will be affected by the changes?
- How has the learning area been defined? Who was involved in the creation or adoption of that definition?
- How will you measure the effectiveness of the changes? What measure will you use (and how will you evaluate its quality)? Who will complete the measure (and under what conditions)?
- What interventions will you use? How were they chosen or developed?
- What evidence do you have to support that these interventions might be effective?
- Who will implement the intervention? How do you plan to prepare these people to deliver the intervention?

These questions will communicate that you are versed in improvement and are eager to understand their process in depth. Speakers who struggle to respond will hopefully become more mindful of such considerations in the future. However, when you hear someone describe a methodologically rigorous and successful learning improvement effort, then as Vanilla Ice says, "stop, collaborate, and listen." This person is a leader in improvement. Learn from them.

Walk the Walk

Changes to the language we use to discuss improvement are important, but we must also change our actions. Each of us needs to seek out learning opportunities, partnerships, and projects that allow us to build our readiness for fostering learning improvement. Strategies to meet this goal will differ depending on institutional roles and prior professional development, but all of us—the authors of this book included—have much work to do.

Our recommendation is that every institution begin their journey into improvement now. No matter your institution's current position, you can contribute to spurring learning improvement efforts. We recommend setting the goal of achieving one legitimate learning improvement example at the program level in the next 5 years.

If you are a faculty member, consider being your program's learning improvement champion. Build your coalition and plan for improvement. Use this book as a guide throughout your journey. If you do not feel comfortable leading an effort, identify someone who might be willing to take the lead and let them know that you'll support them. Faculty are the heart of improvement initiatives. Their proximity to students places them in an optimal position to observe student learning, identify areas in need of improvement, and argue for the importance of coordinated change efforts.

If you are an assessment professional or a faculty developer, we have four suggestions. First: Begin to cross-train and collaborate. As we have discussed at length throughout this book, learning improvement requires considerable skill in multiple domains (Pope & Fulcher, 2019; Reder & Crimmins, 2018). The more you know about each of these domains, the better positioned you will be to guide a learning improvement effort. If you are an assessment professional, learn as much as you can about faculty development. If you are a faculty developer, learn as much as you can about assessment. The most important thing you can do, though, is to develop in-person connections to your colleagues at your institution. If you have not met the assessment professionals or faculty developers on your campus, try to do so. Learn about their work. Collaborate on projects. Fostering ongoing partnerships will help both parties to develop their skills.

Second, begin greasing the wheels for improvement. Ask department heads whether they can identify an area of learning that their unit's instructors would like to improve. During these conversations, try to determine the level of commitment to and enthusiasm for the effort, both from the department head and from the department faculty. If you have the chance, pitch the need to work on learning improvement at scale to senior leadership. Ask what types of support they may be willing to offer. For example, could they encourage participation in a meeting among department heads? Could they provide mini-grants for professional development?

Third, begin providing professional development opportunities on learning improvement at scale. For example, offer a short presentation about the difference between change and improvement. Or, provide a half-day workshop on the basics of learning improvement. Consider holding a book group that reads this book and completes its exercises together. Alternatively, or in addition, consider creating a space where programs can develop their learning improvement ideas. For example, in fall 2019, we facilitated a learning improvement class at JMU, attended by several graduate students (for credit) and a handful of faculty members for their own professional development. As part of the class, two teams incrementally built hypothetical learning improvement plans. The class participants and the instructor critiqued and refined the plans week by week. By the end of the semester, each of the teams had developed a detailed strategy to improve student learning at scale. As we finalize this manuscript, one of the plans has transitioned from a hypothetical exercise into the real world and is in the process of being implemented in our home institution's general education program.

Fourth, and finally, contribute to learning improvement at scale beyond your institution. If you and your colleagues are able to successfully implement an improvement project, share the story with other professionals through conference presentations or through the Learning Improvement Community (n.d.). If you serve on the editorial board of a journal, encourage your colleagues to solicit scholarly articles on learning improvement. The more people who approach learning improvement rigorously, the faster the movement will take hold.

If you are a senior leader on your campus, start by asking yourself this question: Do you spend more time and resources supporting the quality of students' higher education experience or supporting the perception of quality? We've heard the situation posed as follows: If you spend more money on strategic communication than on resources to support teaching and learning, then your quality "talk" is proportionally larger than your quality "walk." If you are in this position, look to get this ratio in better proportion. One strategic way to keep your ratio in check is through a rigorous learning improvement orientation.

Another way you can support learning improvement efforts is by letting people know that you are beginning to pilot projects aimed at improving student learning. If you are responsible for hiring assessment coordinators or faculty developers, include questions about program-level learning improvement in your interviews. Ask if candidates have experience being a part of a learning improvement team and ask them what evidence they have that student learning actually improved. If they have worked on teams that have successfully accomplished learning improvement, move them to the top of your hiring list (assuming they have met your other qualifications, of course!).

If you are part of an accrediting body, we would like to pose three recommendations. As a first step, investigate and revise current standards to use more precise language about improving student learning. Clarity and specificity are crucial. It is preferable to refer to "evidence of logical changes" than "evidence of improvement" if that is what the standards and reviewers are seeking. If truly improved student learning is the goal, though, the standards should outline these expectations clearly.

Second, begin reinforcing improvement efforts. If possible, provide awards or commendations for instances of learning improvement. Begin requesting workshops on improvement at annual conferences and suggest to member institutions that improvement will likely be incorporated into future standards.

Third, make sure that the accreditation staff and reviewers participate in professional development on learning improvement. If learning improvement efforts are to be reinforced and publicized, they must first be properly identified. The gravitas of accreditation language is a strong force on college campuses, so changes to accreditation policies can have significant impacts on university practices and policies.

Future Pathways

The possibilities for a higher education system enriched by regular improvement efforts are an exciting prospect. Although the steps outlined in this book do not make improvement easy, they do provide a road map for planning and implementing improvement efforts, as well as evaluating their effectiveness. Our hope is that the techniques we have discussed will lead to varied improvement efforts, vigorous discussion, and new lessons about how best to tackle the problems posed by a changing world.

We hope our readers will take these lessons and apply them to new areas and new challenges. A prime area for implementing these techniques is the issue of equity in higher education. Discussions about achievement gaps between racial groups, socioeconomic groups, and students pursuing varied educational pathways continue to pose urgent problems for colleges and universities. The tools associated with learning improvement at scale offer methods of studying and remedying inequities in SLOs. For example, an intervention and implementation approach could be pursued with the intended result of reducing a gap in a critical outcome between full-time and part-time students in a given major, or between transfer students and nontransfer students on a particular university-wide outcome. The learning improvement framework provides a way to focus on critical issues of student knowledge and success; although we are not aware of any examples of learning improvement being used to lessen an achievement gap, we see this application as an important opportunity. Questions of equity necessarily call for evaluation of the efficacy of educational systems. This is the same foundation on which the principles of learning improvement rest.

Student partnership is another area worthy of exploration. Throughout the book we have referenced partnerships among faculty, faculty developers, assessment professionals, and administrators. Students could also be powerful partners (Curtis, 2018). They could contribute to learning improvement in several ways. For starters, student effort is critical in their learning. A better learning environment only produces better learning outcomes when students take advantage of it. Students can also provide critical information related to improvement efforts. For example, they can give insider accounts of connections that could be made across courses, identify gaps in their experienced curricula, and provide feedback about skills and knowledge they would like to strengthen.

Finally, we have barely scratched the surface regarding the importance of leadership. Good leaders help establish climate, set priorities, and often can channel resources for learning improvement. This is an area within assessment and improvement that sorely needs more investigation.

Conclusion

Over the past 5 years, we have engaged in many amazing conversations with higher educators who have the will to improve student learning on their campuses. We have spoken to instructors who work tirelessly to make their classes better. We know dozens of faculty developers who take deep pride in helping instructors design and implement better classes. Our colleagues in the assessment profession are constantly strategizing to develop more effective, useful methods of measuring student learning. We see administrators who dream of better-organized, highly effective educational systems. We have collaborated with accreditors who wish to set out policy to propel academe into a brighter future.

While these efforts should be rightfully applauded, we can do better. Professionals in each of these areas—ourselves included—can do a better job integrating our talents and passions. We hope the knowledge, skills, and tools you have acquired through this book help you do your part in building a better higher education system, one where your skills and ideas can be integrated with those of your colleagues and where each generation of students leaves your campus more prepared than the last.

AFTERWORD

Traversing Uncharted Waters

This book offers welcome clarity in language and outlines processes for evidencing learning improvement at scale for the field of assessment in higher education. It unfolds in mostly uncharted waters, leaving opportunities for future scholarship and thought leaders in its wake. To outline several of those opportunities and reinforce the unique position of this book within the discourse of assessment in higher education, this afterword is divided into three sections. The first discusses the alignment of learning improvement with a system view of higher education. The second presents some unanswered questions open for future scholars and learning improvement thought leaders to continue the development of learning improvement model development. The last section builds upon the prior two and presents several future opportunities for learning improvement scholarship and dialogue in higher education and assessment overall.

Alignment With System View

Keston H. Fulcher and Caroline O. Prendergast make the case for working to document learning improvement at scale, where all students in a program are recipients of improved learning. Their focus is on program-level efforts, which require collaboration throughout a department or program, with faculty leading the way toward more intentional educational design. They rightfully concur that change within individual courses is occurring with regularity, but that changes across courses that ultimately coalesce at the program level to impact the entirety of the student learning journey are rare. It is for this reason they focus on learning improvement of all students in a program. This collective-level approach brings an integrated systems lens to the efforts of engaging in learning improvement processes and practices. It also serves as a reminder that the learning outcomes most desired for students (such as critical thinking, effective communication, ethical reasoning) are necessarily acquired when students run into them in various contexts in various courses and experiences. Focusing on horizontal and vertical alignment (Jankowski & Marshall, 2017), mapping, professional development, and implementation fidelity (Finney & Smith, 2016) the authors lead the reader to consider how different pieces operate together as an effective (or ineffective) learning system.

One system-level thread interspersed throughout the book is a focus on design: intentional program design with hallmarks of backward design (Wiggins & McTighe, 2005). Yet, the authors do not stop at design. They embed faculty development and implementation fidelity into the assess, intervene, reassess model to ensure that faculty are equipped to deliver the interventions and that students experience the curriculum as intended. The system lens helps faculty see how they impact the larger system as part of an integrated team by making clear how what they each do in their courses helps support and reinforce student advancement toward shared program-matic learning outcomes.

Within a system, clear definitions and processes are key to effective implementation, a point made by the authors in distinguishing between sim-ply making a change and ultimately improving student learning. Focusing on faculty teams—not individual faculty leading assessment efforts alone or the amorphous "faculty" regularly referred to in writings as a collective that magically advances various initiatives throughout the institution while teaching a full load, engaging in service, and working toward promotion and tenure benchmarks—reinforces the system integration of elements working together through various components that support shared goals.

The system view not only reinforces the role of intentional educational design, but also serves to position learning outcomes as a vital part of the lived experience of a program, where assessment is not just an add on, but a source of information within a program that was intentionally built to achieve them. The authors remind the reader that good assessment is merely a necessary condition for improvement, not a sufficient one, and that higher education needs to be more integrated and thoughtfully designed overall. The focus in the book on avoiding miscommunication is to be applauded along with encouraging the development of connections to colleagues throughout an institution. Further, the authors stress that engaging in learning improvement is time-intensive, unfolding over several years and requiring careful decisions about design issues to remove noise in gathered data on learning, thus also positioning the effort to impact organizational culture and change processes.

The points raised in the book align well with several of the elements of a learning systems paradigm including consensus-based, aligned, and commu-nicated (Jankowski & Marshall, 2017). Consensus-based elements serve to provide clarity on vision and language for a program even though everyone might not agree; alignment entails knowing how the different pieces add up and support the movement toward the goals across courses; communicated involves being clear with each other about what is being done, how, where, and when in the learning environment; and transparent in terms of documenting learning to gather evidence about learning improvement. While these newly charted waters bring clear paths for others to follow, interesting questions remain along with future directions.

Unanswered Questions

Although this book offers an outline on the process of undertaking learning improvement, there are questions yet to be asked and answered and space for clarity, as there is in all models. Scholars and practitioners might consider unpacking some potential assumptions built into the model. For instance, to engage in learning improvement at the program level, does the system view assume the program is a closed unit for purposes of intervention and reassessment? If a biology program engaged in an intervention around writing at the same time as a campus-wide writing initiative with cocurricular and residence hall reinforcement, how much potential improvement should be attributed to which intervention if the student experiences all of them throughout their educational journey? Often throughout higher education institutions, multiple initiatives are underway simultaneously and students do not experience a program in isolation (Kuh et al., 2015). With the distinction between signal and noise raised by the authors, which parts of the educational system are considered "in" versus "out of bounds" in determining improvement impact? A brief sampling of additional questions is offered here to begin mapping the uncharted waters.

How applicable is the assess, intervene, reassess model for community college settings or institutions that predominantly serve adult learners, have a high level of transfer students, or whose students attend part time? The model may be best designed for four-year institutions that serve traditional-age college students who attend full-time, do not transfer, and rarely move between programs upon program selection. To ensure that students experience the curriculum and interventions as intended, in the time period of a cohort, students need to move through the interventions in a timely fashion with a specific cohort. Students who are not in step with their more traditional-aged college peers attending full-time may not experience the intervention as intended. They may instead have extended time between points of measurement of learning due to stopping in and out, course taking patterns, or time required to move through a curriculum by attending part time. They might experience additional external interventions in the cocurriculum or employment, or experience intended programming out of order which may make viewing the program as a closed unit for measurement purposes difficult. Understanding how the model is realized or modified in different institutional contexts is an open opportunity.

How should the tensions between current student programmatic needs and determining learner improvement be balanced? Social science is inherently messy. In education there is limited opportunity to control for various factors throughout the entirety of the educational environment. Further, educators desire to help students be successful. This combination makes holding a program steady until reassessment somewhat difficult in relation to the tensions of supporting student attainment of learning outcomes and methodological desires to evidence learning improvement. How should the focus upon measuring quality of program design be balanced with faculty noticing that an intervention is not working partway through implementation and desiring to make changes before a cohort graduates still weak in a particular learning outcome? The tension between evidencing learning improvement and educating students across a program once program-wide conversations begin may prove difficult, but an opportunity for better understanding faculty programmatic change efforts and practices.

Where should equity be considered in the learning improvement model in root cause analysis and intervention selection? While there is much to applaud in basing interventions on existing theory and research, there are systematic issues at play that limit the research base, which theories are published, what gets researched, and for whom intervention literature exists (Montenegro & Jankowski, 2020). Employing research findings that are not a good fit for a particular student population or trying to find research to support an intervention for a student population that is rarely studied or has limited published theory or research does not mean that the process halts. It does however mean there is an opportunity to consider the role of students in commenting on the root cause of a situation and/or what intervention the students might recommend a program employ. Student involvement in assessment can also help determine baseline learning and environmental factors and assist in determining which components are controllable within the program, which may be outside the jurisdiction of the program but within the institutional learning system, and which may even be the result of systemic racism (Jankowski et al., 2020). The voice of students can help to interrupt faculty bias or assumptions, as can looking to the margins for silenced voices to provide guidance to programmatic learning improvement. The case of educational responses to COVID-19 is an example of a need to involve student voices (Jankowski, 2020), but also one that can disrupt holding a program constant for evidencing learning improvement. Investigating the literature bases examined and needed by faculty to engage in equitable learning improvement is an opportunity to explore.

Which faculty have input into the process and in what ways should faculty-led learning improvement protect junior faculty? To be truly collaborative, learning improvement efforts should ideally involve a combination of senior and junior faculty working together to design a successful program. The authors state that faculty engagement does not mean everyone has to participate, which is welcome news indeed. But, in departments where there is one faculty member and many adjuncts, who does the work? How are interventions communicated to adjunct faculty, or to faculty whose professional development is part of a negotiated union contract? Should there be consideration within the model of the human, cultural, political, governance, and structural differences throughout the diverse system of higher education? Not every program and faculty has the same control over programs as others to determine and implement interventions. Further, how might academic leadership reassure faculty participating in learning improvement that data on faculty member's effectiveness in teaching a specific learning outcome will not be used punitively? And while learning improvement requires widescale professional development, does it also require a different faculty role in higher education? Or different graduate preparation and hiring practices for future faculty? Unpacking faculty roles in leading improvement efforts within different institutional models will help provide examples for various programmatic structures and types on how to engage in the work.

Future Opportunities

It is my hope that the prior questions led the reader to see how needed the goal of this book is in terms of adding clarity to evidencing learning improvement. To reach the goals outlined by the authors for the future of higher education, there are several key opportunities for scholars. Although the unanswered questions serve as indicators that there is much excitement and opportunity to engage in further defining learning improvement, the learning improvement community is an open one that is welcoming of additional voices, considerations, and perspectives. Some spaces for involvement are shared next.

Additional models. The learning improvement model is an overarching model or framework, but that means there is space for other models within that are unique or specific to different institutional types, governance structures, and faculty administration. The focus in the book is on a learning improvement mindset, so determining how such a mindset might materialize within different institutions is rife with possibilities.

Literature connections. Connecting the learning improvement model to other literature bases, such as change management, may provide readily available solutions to help programs in process stay the course through leadership changes, new initiatives, and issues that arise in uncertain times. Permanence is not something we have the luxury to assume within higher education programs at the moment, and positioning learning improvement as a means to build a productive future may serve to ensure durability in the short term.

Narrative analysis. The stance of learning improvement raised by this book comes from the desire for better intentional educational design that is undertaken in alignment with the vision that the role and purpose of higher education is to ensure students acquire the desired learning by the end. It is about the process of being critical, intentional, and committed to ensuring learning is actually improving for all students over time.

Within higher education there have not been stories of learning improvement because it was not a narrative trying to be told. If the process of assessment was about external accountability reporting, the point was to provide evidence of being accountable and engaging in the regular and ongoing process of assessment. The narrative was that assessment was unfolding with regularity, not about improving student learning.

For too long, assessment in higher education did not have examples of follow-up to track changes in improvement because it was not asked of them. Accrediting and reporting related forms desired to see a process of continuously examining student learning with documented changes, but just because no one asked to see if the changes led to improvements does not mean the question should not have been asked ourselves. Sharing narratives and becoming clearer about learning improvement narratives is a welcome future opportunity to refine and guide efforts.

Last Words

This book reminds us that starting with articulating a shared problem that is noticeable and collectively owned across the faculty of a program is more likely to have an impact on student learning than simply engaging in assessment with regularity—a point similarly made by Kuh et al. (2015) on how to foster meaningful use. Finding something shared, something common, and something that is agreed upon where students collectively struggle means the program is more likely to succeed in addressing it. We are all trying to make arguments about programs, institutions, and learning—that a specific environment and intervention led to the learning seen at the end. Making a learning improvement claim means providing an evidenced argument about how a program and the students that experienced the program achieved learning. An argumentative stance is found in evidence-based storytelling (Jankowski, 2021) where the focus is on a warrant that provides supporting evidence for the argument, drawing threads between what is done and related impacts seen on student learning. It is that goal to which we strive and why it is important to unpack what is meant by learning improvement, especially for the discipline of assessment which defines itself in part as improving student learning. This book sets us on a much-needed path of exploration.

Natasha A. Jankowski PhD
Executive Director,
National Institute for Learning Outcomes Assessment (NILOA)

Student Affairs Learning Improvement Example

The following story is based on the real-life learning improvement example from James Madison University's (JMU's) Transfer Orientation program. This work received the 2012 NASPA Grand Gold Excellence award. We modified details to make the narrative more congruent with the steps laid out in this book. For more information about the Transfer Orientation project see National Association of Student Personnel Administration (n.d.) and Gerstner and Finney (2013).

JMU's academic advisers and staff in the registrar's office recognized that many transfer students were unaware of academic requirements deep into their college experience. As the number of new transfer students increased, JMU decided that specific strategies were needed to support their success. A logical place to start was the orientation office. This unit already had created an effective orientation for all full-time, first-time students, and they had recently begun programming that reached all transfer students. In other words, the orientation office could affect student learning and development at scale. Many implementers of the transfer program were part of the orientation office, and the culture of office employees was highly collaborative.

Furthermore, the orientation office had fostered relationships with several key partners across the university. The assessment office, the registrar's office, and the general education program were willing to work together if it meant better outcomes for the transfer students. Early in the process, the group worked to carefully articulate the intended student learning outcome (SLO). After many iterations, the group adopted the following statement:

> After attending [transfer orientation] students will be able to correctly identify the academic requirements for major, degree, and graduation completion at JMU.

For example, did students know how many credits are needed to graduate? Could they identify how many credits could be transferred from other institutions? This information was critical for student success at the university.

Given that the answers to these questions were JMU specific, the orientation team created an eight-item multiple-choice test about academic requirements in coordination with the assessment office. For example, one such item was

What is the minimum number of credit hours all students must complete in order to receive a degree from JMU?

a. 115
b. 120 (correct answer)
c. 125
d. 130

After transfer orientation, students completed a battery of surveys and tests. One part of the assessment included the academic requirements test. Students averaged 76% correct (baseline student performance), considerably lower than the 90% the orientation office had hoped to see. The orientation leaders and assessment experts began exploring why the transfer students were performing lower than expected by examining the learning environment. A first step was examining the curriculum map, which suggested that students should receive the appropriate information during their orientation process.

The existing intervention strategy included a representative from the registrar's office explaining various requirements. Although the speaker was dynamic, the delivery format was essentially a lecture with key information being delivered only once.

Upon investigating the baseline conditions, the orientation team decided that the interventions could be modified by taking tips from cognitive science. As opposed to straight lecture, the presenter could pepper the lecture with questions and have students respond to him. He could correct students if they were wrong. In essence, he would use the first tip provided by Halpern and Hakel (2003): Students are more likely to retain information long term when they are given practice at retrieval.

The representative from the registrar's office now had a new game plan. His presentation not only covered the material on academic requirements, but also incorporated directed questions and answers to cue students' practice and retrieval. Members of the assessment office were asked to conduct implementation fidelity checks during the academic requirement presentation. Indeed, the implementer stuck to the plan, covering the necessary material and using the new presentation technique. Furthermore, the incoming transfer students were visibly more engaged than the previous cohort had been during the presentation.

Finally, it was time to examine the responses from students who had experienced the new version of transfer orientation. It was the moment of truth. Was the modified intervention more effective? The average reassessment score was 86%, a moderately positive effect, and statistically significant relative to the previous year's 76% average score. Despite falling just short of the desired outcome of 90%, there was little doubt that the change to the learning environment produced the improvement in SLOs.

Abridged Learning Improvement at Scale Proposal for the
Psychology BA Program

Submitted by Xela Baker and Rusty Schomburg

1. Program name: Psychology BA
2. Number of program graduates per year: ~300 students
3. How many faculty members/instructors teach in the program? Please list the number of full-time tenured/tenure-track faculty, full-time instructors (non-tenure-track), and adjunct instructors.

   50 instructors teach in the psychology program:

   - Full-time tenured or tenure-track: 30
   - Full-time instructors (non-tenure-track): 5
   - Adjunct: 15

4. What is the area you wish to improve and why is it important?

   We desire to improve our students' writing skills. More specifically, we have recently noticed that students in our program struggle to select appropriate writing strategies when faced with a specific writing context. For example, we frequently find students unable to differentiate between the expectations of basic response papers and formal scientific research papers. We are concerned that a lack of familiarity with selecting and executing appropriate approaches to writing will hinder our graduates' career prospects. However, if we are able to transform the way we teach them to approach writing, we believe that they will enter graduate school and/or the workforce with a distinct advantage. Writing, in its various forms, permeates all of our professional lives. If we can help our students to transform this skill from a barrier into a strength, we will be providing them with lifelong tools while boosting the reputation of our program.

5. Who is/are the champion(s) for this effort and what relevant skills/knowledge do they have for this improvement effort?

   Xela Baker and Rusty Schomburg will act as cochampions for the initiative. Both have taught in the psychology program for over 10 years.

For the past 6 years, Xela has served as the assessment coordinator, which has provided her with basic skills in academic measurement and assessment. Additionally, Xela has collaborated with almost half of the instructors in the department on various initiatives over the past decade. The partnerships she has built during these projects will be important tools for gathering allies throughout the learning improvement process.

Rusty has taught in the psychology program for close to 20 years. He has led multiple large initiatives to great success within the department, and he has won multiple awards for teaching and mentorship. His previous leadership roles have prepared him to navigate the departmental politics of change initiatives.

Both Rusty and Xela have participated in course redesign workshops offered by the university's teaching excellence center in the past 5 years.

6. What courses will likely be changed in support of this project? Please note whether the courses are electives or required courses. If the course is an elective, please provide an estimated proportion of the number of students who complete the course during the program. Additionally, please provide the number of the faculty/instructors who teach each course and identify any steps that have been taken thus far to elicit their collaboration.

We have identified three required courses that would be good candidates for a writing intervention:

- PSYC 201: An introductory-level research methods class (10 sections taught annually; five instructors teach two sections apiece)
- PSYC 310: A course on careers in psychology usually taken during students' junior year (10 sections taught annually; five instructors teach two sections apiece)
- PSYC 495: The senior-year capstone course (15 sections taught annually; five instructors teach three sections apiece)

We have discussed the potential for a learning improvement initiative with each of the instructors for these courses. The 15 instructors who are responsible for teaching these courses have agreed to participate in the initiative if we are selected for further support.

7. What are your initial ideas regarding interventions intended to improve the targeted learning area?

Generally, we believe the problem stems from the current lack of specific writing instruction in our curriculum. We assumed that students would learn to identify the requirements of different types of writing because they were exposed to different types of writing in their classes. However, without explicit instruction, it seems that students are missing key features of different styles and approaches. Our introductory literature review seems to indicate that students become better writers when they are able to deconstruct and analyze the stylistic "moves" made by other authors; this then allows them to purposefully select techniques to use in their own writing. Therefore, our initial idea is to develop interventions targeting students' ability to identify the context in which writing is occurring, evaluate the effectiveness of different stylistic approaches, and "translate" the same content between different writing contexts.

8. What is the anticipated timeline?

- Year 1: Define area, select/create instruments, collect baseline data.
- Year 2: Develop interventions, pilot in select classes, train up all faculty in the intervention chain.
- Year 3: Deploy interventions across all classes (most graduating seniors will receive intervention in one course).
- Year 4: Deploy interventions across all classes (most graduating seniors will receive intervention in two courses).
- Year 5: Deploy interventions across all classes (all graduating seniors will receive intervention in all three courses).

Note

This example is a shortened version of JMU's Learning Improvement by Design Request for Proposals form (Fulcher & Meixner, n.d.). The full version of the form can be found here: https://www.jmu.edu/learningimprovement/learning-improvement-by-design/learning-improvement-rfp.shtml

APPENDIX C

Sample Implementation Fidelity Checklist

| Objective | Program component | Exposure | | Specific features | Adherence (yes/no) | Quality: 1 = Low (confusing), 3 = Medium, 5 = High (clear) | Responsiveness: 1 = Low (unengaged), 3 = Medium, 5 = High (engaged) |
		Planned	Actual				
		25 min		In groups, students examine three different artifacts referring to the same topic (a TED Talk, a newspaper article, and a journal abstract). Students generate a list of similarities and differences between the artifacts.			
SLO 1	Activity	25 min		Using the lists created in the first part of the activity, the whole class (guided by the instructor) engages in a discussion about why the artifacts differ.			

(Continues)

(*Continued*)

| Objective | Program component | Exposure | | Specific features | Adherence (yes/no) | Quality: 1 = Low (confusing), 3 = Medium, 5 = High (clear) | Responsiveness: 1 = Low (unengaged), 3 = Medium, 5 = High (engaged) |
		Planned	Actual				
	Lecture	50 min		Instructor provides a lecture-based lesson about the history of scientific communication, emphasizing why certain stylistic choices (e.g., citations, direct quotations, passive voice, and first-person language) are or are not common in given types of communication.			
SLO 2	Assignment	75 min		As an out-of-class assignment, students create concept maps illustrating the relationships among multiple types of writing (e.g., cover letters, formal emails, journal articles) and their features and purposes.			
	Activity	50 min		Each student gives a brief presentation of their final concept map.			

Note: SLO 1 concerns students' ability to recognize the elements of a writing context that influence appropriate choice of writing strategy. SLO 2 concerns students' ability to explain the reasons for differences among written communication styles relevant to psychological research, scientific communication, and professional workplaces. More information about the SLOs and interventions can be found in chapter 2.

American Educational Research Association, American Psychological Association, & National Council on Measurement in Education. (2014). *Standards for educational and psychological testing.* American Educational Research Association.

Angelo, T. A. (1999). Doing assessment as if learning matters most. *AAHE Bulletin, 51*(9), 3–6. https://www.aahea.org/articles/angelomay99.htm

Angelo, T. A. (2000). Doing faculty development as if we value learning most: Transformative guidelines from research and practice. In D. Lieberman & C. M. Wehlburg (Eds.) *To Improve the Academy* (Vol. 19, 97–112). Bolton, MA: Anker.

Angelo, T. A., & Cross, K. P. (1993). *Classroom assessment techniques: A handbook for college teachers.* Jossey-Bass.

Appleby, D. C., & Appleby, K. M. (2006). Kisses of death in the graduate school application process. *Teaching of Psychology, 33*(1), 19–24. https://doi.org/10.1207/s15328023top3301_5

Astin, A. W. (1985). *Achieving educational excellence: A critical assessment of priorities and practices in higher education.* Jossey-Bass.

Baker, G. R., Jankowski, N. A., Provezis, S., & Kinzie, J. (2012, July). *Using assessment results: Promising practices of institutions that do it well.* University of Illinois and Indiana University, National Institute for Learning Outcomes Assessment.

Bandalos, D. L. (2018). *Measurement theory and applications for the social sciences.* Guilford.

Banta, T. W. (2007). Can assessment for accountability complement assessment for improvement? *Peer Review, 9*(2), 9–12. https://www.aacu.org/publications-research/periodicals/can-assessment-accountability-complement-assessment-improvement

Banta, T. W., & Blaich, C. (2011). Closing the assessment loop. *Change: The Magazine of Higher Learning, 43*(1), 22–27. https://doi.org/ 10.1080/00091383.2011.538642

Beach, A. L., Sorcinelli, M. D., Austin, A. E., & Rivard, J. K. (2016). *Faculty development in the age of evidence: Current practices, future imperatives.* Stylus.

Beaton, A. E., & Zwick, R. (1990). *The effect of changes in the national assessment: Disentangling the NAEP 1985–86 reading anomaly* (NAEP Report no. 17–TR–21). Educational Testing Service.

Bok, D. (2008). *Our underachieving colleges: A candid look at how much students learn and why they should be learning more.* Princeton University Press.

Breitenstein, S. M., Gross, D., Garvey, C. A., Hill, C., Fogg, L., & Resnick, B. (2010). Implementation fidelity in community-based interventions. *Research in Nursing & Health, 33*(2), 164–173. https://doi.org/10.1002/nur.20373

Brown, S., & Knight, P. (1994). *Assessing learners in higher education.* Kogan Page.

Bryk, A. S., Gomez, L. M., Grunow, A., & LeMahieu, P. G. (2017). *Learning to improve: How America's schools can get better at getting better.* Harvard Education Press.

Carnegie Foundation for the Advancement of Teaching (n.d.). *Our ideas: Using improvement science to accelerate learning and address problems of practice.* https://www.carnegiefoundation.org/our-ideas/

Charles Atlas Ltd. (1952). *Hey skinny! . . . Yer ribs are showing!* [Comic book advertisement]. Heritage Auctions. https://comics.ha.com/itm/golden-age-1938-1955-/horror/adventures-into-the-unknown-29-davis-crippen-d-copy-pedigree-acg-1952-cgc-nm-94-off-white-pages/a/18052-12026.s?ic16=ViewItem-Auction-Archive-PreviousPricesHeritage-081514#

Condon, W., Iverson, E. R., Manduca, C. A., Rutz, C., & Willett, G. (2016). *Faculty development and student learning: Assessing the connections.* Indiana University Press.

Connelly, L. M. (2019). Intervention fidelity. *MEDSURG Nursing, 28*(4), 262–263.

Council of Regional Accrediting Commissions. (n.d.). *Who we are.* https://www.c-rac.org/copy-of-about-us

Crocker, L. (2003). Teaching for the test: Validity, fairness, and moral action. *Educational Measurement: Issues and Practice, 22*(3), 5–11. https://doi.org/10.1111/j.1745-3992.2003.tb00132.x

Curtis, N. A. (2018). *A new paradigm for improvement: Student-faculty partnership in learning outcomes assessment* (Publication No. 10809551) [Doctoral dissertation, James Madison University]. ProQuest Dissertations and Theses Global.

Daly, M. C., & Bengali, L. (2014, May 5). *Is it still worth going to college?* Federal Reserve Bank of San Francisco. https://www.frbsf.org/economic-research/publications/economic-letter/2014/may/is-college-worth-it-education-tuition-wages/

Dane, A. V., & Schneider, B. H. (1998). Program integrity in primary and early secondary prevention: Are implementation effects out of control? *Clinical Psychology Review, 18*(1), 23–45. https://doi.org/10.1016/S0272-7358(97)00043-3

Daniel, F., Gaze, C. M., & Braasch, J. L. G. (2015). Writing cover letters that address instructor feedback improves final papers in a research methods course. *Teaching of Psychology, 42*(1), 64–68. https://doi.org/10.1177/0098628314562680

Dewey, J. (1923). *Democracy and education: An introduction to the philosophy of education.* Macmillan.

Dhillon, S., Darrow, C., & Meyers, C. V. (2015). Introduction to implementation fidelity. In C. V. Meyers and W. C. Brandt (Eds.), *Implementation fidelity in education research* (pp. 8–22). Routledge.

Dickson, K. L., & Treml, M. M. (2013). Using assessment and SoTL to enhance student learning. In R. A. R. Gurung & J. H. Wilson (Eds.), *Doing the scholarship of teaching and learning: Measuring systematic changes to teaching and improvements in learning* (New Directions for Teaching and Learning, no. 136, pp. 7–16). Jossey-Bass. https://doi.org/10.1002/tl.20072

Educational Testing Services. (n.d.). *HEIghten® outcomes assessment suite research.* https://www.ets.org/heighten/research/

Evans, C. (2013). Making sense of assessment feedback in higher education. *Review of Educational Research, 83*(1), 70–120. https://doi.org/10.3102/0034654312474350

Ewell, P. T. (2002). An emerging scholarship: A brief history of assessment. In T. W. Banta (Ed.), *Building a scholarship of assessment* (pp. 3–25). Jossey-Bass.

Ewell, P. T. (2009). *Assessment, accountability, and improvement: Revisiting the tension* (NILOA Occasional Paper no.1). University of Illinois and Indiana University, National Institute for Learning Outcomes Assessment.

Filer, K., & Steehler, G. (2018). Lessons learned from a decade of authentic assessment. *Peer Review, 20*(4), 15–17.

Fink, L. D. (2013). *Creating significant learning experiences: An integrated approach to designing college courses.* Wiley.

Finney, S. J., & Smith, K. L. (2016, January). Ignorance is not bliss: Implementation fidelity and learning improvement. *Viewpoint.* National Institute for Learning Outcomes Assessment. https://www.learningoutcomesassessment.org/wp-ontent/uploads/2019/08/Viewpoint-FinneySmith.pdf

Fisher, R., Smith, K., Finney, S., & Pinder, K. (2014). The importance of implementation fidelity data for evaluating program effectiveness. *About Campus, 19*(5), 28–32. https://doi.org/10.1002/abc.21171

Fulcher, K. H., Good, M. R., Coleman, C. M., & Smith, K. L. (2014, December). *A simple model for learning improvement: Weigh pig, feed pig, weigh pig* (Occasional Paper no. 23). University of Illinois and Indiana University, National Institute for Learning Outcomes Assessment.

Fulcher, K., & Meixner, C. (n.d.). *JMU learning improvement: Request for proposals.* James Madison University. https://www.jmu.edu/learningimprovement/learning-improvement-by-design/learning-improvement-rfp.shtml

Fulcher, K. H., & Prendergast, C. O. (2019). Lots of assessment, little improvement? How to fix the broken system. In S. P. Hundley & S. Kahn (Eds.), *Trends in assessment: Ideas, opportunities, and issues for higher education.* Stylus.

Fulcher, K. H., Smith, K. L., Sanchez, E. R., Ames, A. J., & Meixner, C. (2017). Return of the pig: Standards for learning improvement. *Research & Practice in Assessment, 11*, 10–40. https://files.eric.ed.gov/fulltext/EJ1137991.pdf

Fulcher, K. H., & Willse, J. T. (2007). Value added: Back to basics in measuring change. *Assessment Update, 19*(5), 10–12. https://doi.org/10.1002/au

Gerstner, J. J., & Finney, S. J. (2013). Measuring the implementation fidelity of student affairs programs: A critical component of the outcomes assessment cycle. *Research & Practice in Assessment, 8*, 15–28. https://www.rpajournal.com/dev/wp-content/uploads/2013/11/SF2.pdf

Gilbert, E. (2015, August 14). Does assessment make colleges better? Who knows? *The Chronicle of Higher Education.* https://www.chronicle.com/article/does-assessment-make-colleges-better-who-knows/

Gilbert, E. (2018, January 12). An insider's take on assessment: It may be worse than you thought. *The Chronicle of Higher Education*. https://www.chronicle.com/article/an-insiders-take-on-assessment-it-may-be-worse-than-you-thought/

Good, M. R. (2015). *Improving student learning in higher education: A mixed methods study* (Publication No. 3702665) [Doctoral dissertation, James Madison University]. ProQuest Dissertations and Theses Global.

Haladyna, T. M., Downing, S. M., & Rodriguez, M. C. (2002). A review of multiple-choice item-writing guidelines for classroom assessment. *Applied Measurement in Education, 15*(3), 309–333. https://doi.org/10.1207/S15324818AME1503_5

Halpern, D. F., & Hakel, M. D. (2003). Applying the science of learning to the university and beyond: Teaching for long-term retention and transfer. *Change: The Magazine of Higher Learning, 35*(4), 36–41. https://doi.org/10.1080/00091380309604109

Hanushek, E. A., & Woessmann, L. (2010). Education and economic growth. In D. J. Brewer and P. J. McEwan (Eds.), *Economics of education* (pp. 60–67). Elsevier. http://hanushek.stanford.edu/sites/default/files/publications/Hanushek%2BWoessmann%202010%20IntEncEduc%202.pdf

Horst, S. J., & Ames, A. J. (2018). Bringing together assessment and learning improvement: Dreaming big for an inaugural summit. *Research & Practice in Assessment, 13*, 6–10. http://www.rpajournal.com/dev/wp-content/uploads/2019/02/W18_A1.pdf

Huber, M. T., & Morreale, S. P. (Eds.) (2002). *Disciplinary styles in the scholarship of teaching and learning: Exploring common ground*. Stylus.

Hulleman, C. S., & Cordray, D. S. (2009). Moving from the lab to the field: The role of fidelity and achieved relative intervention strength. *Journal of Research on Educational Effectiveness, 2*(1), 88–110. https://doi.org/ 10.1080/19345740802539325

Hutchings, P., & Marchese, T. W. (1990). Watching assessment: Questions, stories, prospects. *Change: The Magazine of Higher Learning, 22*(5), 12–38. https://doi.org/10.1080/00091383.1990.9937653

Ishak, S., & Salter, N. P. (2017). Undergraduate psychological writing: A best practices guide and national survey. *Teaching of Psychology, 44*(1), 5–17. https://doi.org/10.1177/0098628316677491

Jankowski, N. A. (2020, August). *Assessment during a crisis: Responding to a global pandemic*. University of Illinois and Indiana University, National Institute for Learning Outcomes Assessment.

Jankowski, N. A. (2021, February). *Evidence-based storytelling in assessment*. (Occasional Paper No. 50). University of Illinois and Indiana University, National Institute for Learning Outcomes Assessment.

Jankowski, N. A., Brown-Tess, K., Baker, G. R., & Montenegro, E. (Eds.). (2020). *Student-focused learning and assessment: Involving students in the learning process in higher education*. Peter Lang.

Jankowski, N. A., & Marshall, D. W. (2017). *Degrees that matter: Moving higher education to a learning systems paradigm*. Stylus.

Jankowski, N. A., Timmer, J. D., Kinzie, J., & Kuh, G. D. (2018, January). *Assessment that matters: Trending toward practices that document authentic student learning.* University of Illinois and Indiana University, National Institute for Learning Outcomes Assessment.

Kahneman, D. (2011). *Thinking, fast and slow.* Farrar, Straus and Giroux.

Kinzie, J., Landy, K., Sorcinelli, M. D., & Hutchings, P. (2019). Better together: How faculty development and assessment can join forces to improve student learning. *Change: The Magazine of Higher Learning, 51*(5), 46–54. https://doi.org/10.1080/00091383.2019.1652076

Kuh, G. D., Ikenberry, S. O., Jankowski, N. A., Cain, T. R., Ewell, P., Hutchings, P., & Kinzie, K. (2015). *Using evidence of student learning to improve higher education.* Jossey-Bass.

Layton, L. (2015). Study: Billions of dollars in annual teacher training is largely a waste. *Washington Post.* https://www.washingtonpost.com/local/education/study-billions-of-dollars-in-annual-teacher-training-is-largely-a-waste/2015/08/03/c4e1f322-39ff-11e5-9c2d-ed991d848c48_story.html

Learning Improvement Community (n.d.). *About us.* https://www.learning-improvement.org/about-us

Lending, D., Fulcher, K. H., Ezell, J. D., May, J. L., & Dillon, T. W. (2018). Example of a program-level learning improvement report. *Research & Practice in Assessment, 13,* 34–50.

Lewis, K. G. (2010). Pathways toward improving teaching and learning in higher education: International context and background. In J. McDonald & D. Stockley (Eds.), *Pathways to the profession of educational development* (New Directions for Teaching and Learning, no. 122, pp. 13–23). Jossey-Bass. https://doi.org/10.1002/tl.394

Lissitz, R. W. (Ed.). (2009). *The concept of validity.* Information Age.

Lyons, J., & Polychronopoulos, G. (2018, June). Triennial assessment as an alternative to annual assessment. University of Illinois and Indiana University, National Institute for Learning Outcomes Assessment.

Maki, P. L. (2017). *Real-time student assessment: Meeting the imperative for improved time to degree, closing the opportunity gap, and assuring student competencies for 21st-century needs.* Stylus.

Mastacusa, E. J., Snyder, W. J., & Hoyt, B. S. (2011). *Effective instruction for STEM disciplines: From learning theory to college teaching.* Jossey-Bass.

Matlin, M. W. (2002). Cognitive psychology and college-level pedagogy: Two siblings that rarely communicate. In D. F. Halpern & M. D. Hakel (Eds.), *Applying the science of learning to university teaching and beyond* (New Directions for Teaching and Learning, no. 89, pp. 87–103). Jossey-Bass. https://doi.org/10.1002/tl.49

McKee, C. W., Johnson, M., Ritchie, W. F., & Tew, W. M. (2013). Professional development of the faculty: Past and present. In C. W. McKee (Ed.), *The breadth of current faculty development: Practitioners' perspectives* (New Directions for Teaching and Learning, no. 133, pp. 15–20). Jossey-Bass. https://doi.org/10.1002/tl.20042

Mertens, D. M., & Wilson, A. T. (2012). *Program evaluation theory and practice: A comprehensive guide.* Guilford.

Montenegro, E., & Jankowski, N. A. (2020, January). *A new decade for assessment: Embedding equity into assessment praxis* (Occasional Paper No. 42). University of Illinois and Indiana University, National Institute for Learning Outcomes Assessment.

Murphy, S. L., & Gutman, S. A. (2012). Intervention fidelity: A necessary aspect of intervention effectiveness studies. *The American Journal of Occupational Therapy, 66*(4), 387–388. https://doi.org/10.5014/ajot.2010.005405

National Association of Student Personnel Administration. (n.d.). *Implementation fidelity and outcomes assessment for transfer orientation: Making empirically-based decision about program effectiveness.* https://www.naspa.org/images/uploads/main/Gold1104.pdf

National Center for Education Statistics. (2020). *Characteristics of postsecondary faculty.* https://nces.ed.gov/programs/coe/indicator_csc.asp

North, J., & Scholl, S. C. (1979). POD: The founding of a national network. *POD Quarterly, 6,* 10–17.

Pope, A. M., & Fulcher, K. H. (2019). Organizing for learning improvement: What it takes. *Assessment Update, 31*(3), 1–2, 15–16. https://doi.org/10.1002/au.30170

Prendergast, C., & Fulcher, K. (2019). *In defense of standardization: Let us move on to an actual villain.* Association for the Assessment of Learning in Higher Education: Emerging Dialogues in Assessment. https://www.aalhe.org/page/ed_2019_indefenseofstandardization

Ray, J., & Kafka, S. (2014, May 6). *Life in college matters for life after college.* Gallup. https://news.gallup.com/poll/168848/life-college-matters-life-college.aspx

Reder, M., & Crimmins, C. (2018). Why assessment and faculty development need each other: Notes on using evidence to improve student learning. *Research & Practice in Assessment, 13,* 15–19.

Rhodes, T. (2010). *Assessing outcomes and improving achievement: Tips and tools for using rubrics.* Association of American Colleges & Universities.

Sanchez, E. R. H., Fulcher, K. H., Smith, K. L., Ames, A., & Hawk, W. J. (2017). Defining, teaching, and assessing ethical reasoning in action. *Change: The Magazine of Higher Learning, 49*(2), 30–36. https://doi.org/10.1080/00091383.2017.1286215

Schmeiser, C. B., & Welch, C. J. (2006). Test development. In R. L. Brennan (Ed.), *Educational measurement* (pp. 307–353). Praeger.

Shadish, W. R., Cook, T. D., & Campbell, D. T. (2002). *Experimental and quasi-experimental designs for generalized causal inference.* Houghton Mifflin.

Sitko, B. M. (1998). Knowing how to write: Metacognition and writing instruction. In D. J. Hacker, J. Dunlosky, & A. C. Graesser (Eds.), *Metacognition in educational theory and practice* (pp. 93–115). Erlbaum.

Smith, K. (2017). *Integrating implementation fidelity and learning improvement to enhance students' ethical reasoning abilities* (Publication No. 10271289) [Doctoral dissertation, James Madison University]. ProQuest Dissertations and Theses Global.

Smith, K. L, Finney, S. J., & Fulcher, K. H. (2019). Connecting assessment practices with curricula and pedagogy via implementation fidelity data. *Assessment and Evaluation in Higher Education, 44*(2), 262–280. https://doi.org/10.1080/0260 2938.2018.1496321

Smith, K. L., Good, M. R., Sanchez, E. H., & Fulcher, K. H. (2015). Communication is key: Unpacking "use of assessment results to improve student learning." *Research & Practice in Assessment, 10,* 15–29.

Steinert, Y., Mann, K., Anderson, B., Barnett, B. M., Centeno, A., Naismith, L., Prideaux, D., Spencer, J., Tullo, E., Viggiano. T., Ward, H., & Dolmans, D. (2016). A systematic review of faculty development initiatives designed to enhance teaching effectiveness: A 10-year update: BEME Guide No. 40. *Medical Teacher, 38*(8), 769–786. https://doi.org/10.1080/0142159x.2016.1181851

Stiggins, R. J. (1987). Design and development of performance assessments. *Educational measurement: Issues and practice, 6*(3), 33–42. https://doi.org/10.1111/j.1745-3992.1987.tb00507.x

Strauss, V. (2014, March 1). Why most professional development for teachers is useless. *Washington Post.* https://www.washingtonpost.com/news/answer-sheet/wp/2014/03/01/why-most-professional-development-for-teachers-is-useless/

Study Group on the Conditions of Excellence in American Higher Education. (1984). *Involvement in learning: Realizing the potential of American higher education: Final report of the study group on the conditions of excellence in American higher education.* U.S. Department of Education.

Sundre, D. L., & Thelk, A. D. (2010). Advancing assessment of quantitative and scientific reasoning. *Numeracy, 3*(2), 1–12. https://doi.org/10.5038/1936-4660.3.2.2

Swain, M. S., Finney, S. J., & Gerstner, J. J. (2013). A practical approach to assessing implementation fidelity. *Assessment Update, 25*(1), 5–13. https://doi.org/10.1002/au.251

Thelin, J. R., & Hirschy, A. S. (2009). College students and the curriculum: The fantastic voyage of higher education, 1636 to the present. *National Academic Advising Association Journal, 29*(2), 9–17. https://doi.org/10.12930/0271-9517-29.2.9

Toomey, E., & Hardeman, W. (2017). Addressing intervention fidelity within physical therapy research and clinical practice. *Journal of Orthopedic Sports Physical Therapy, 47*(12), 895–898. https://doi.org/ 10.2519/jospt.2017.0609

Trostel, P. (2015). *It's not just the money: The benefits of college education to individuals and to society.* Lumina Foundation.

U.S. Department of Education. (2006). *A test of leadership: Charting the future of U.S. higher education.* Author.

Warren, J. (1984). The blind alley of value added. *American Association for Higher Education Bulletin, 37*(1), 10–13. https://www.learningoutcomesassessment.org/wp-content/uploads/2019/08/Warren-BlindAlley.pdf

Wiggins, G., & McTighe, J. (2005). *Understanding by design* (2nd ed.). Association for Supervision and Curriculum Development.

Worthen, M. (2018, February 23). The misguided drive to measure "learning outcomes." *New York Times.* https://www.nytimes.com/2018/02/23/opinion/sunday/colleges-measure-learning-outcomes.html

Zvoch, K. (2012). How does fidelity of implementation matter? Using multilevel models to detect relationships between participant outcomes and the delivery and receipt of treatment. *American Journal of Evaluation, 33*(4), 547–565. https://doi.org/ 10.1177/1098214012452715

ABOUT THE AUTHORS

Keston H. Fulcher is the executive director of the Center for Assessment and Research Studies and professor in graduate psychology at James Madison University (JMU). JMU has received an unprecedented 14 national recognitions related to student learning outcomes assessment. Fulcher's research focuses on structuring higher education for learning improvement. He serves on the advisory panel to the National Institute for Learning Outcomes Assessment, collaborates extensively with the Assessment Institute in Indianapolis, and is one of the founders of the Learning Improvement Community.

Caroline O. Prendergast is completing her PhD in Assessment and Measurement at James Madison University (JMU). She has 6 years of experience in educational assessment, ranging from international large-scale assessment to work with small student affairs programs in higher education. Her current work involves providing assessment-related training and resources to faculty and staff across JMU's campus and beyond and partnering with academic programs to pursue large-scale learning improvement projects. Her research primarily concerns the role of assessment in promoting the improvement of student learning.

(Continued from preceding page)

Transforming Digital Learning and Assessment

A Guide to Available and Emerging Practices and Building Institutional Consensus

Edited by Peggy L. Maki and Peter Shea

Foreword by Bryan Alexander

"Maki and Shea brilliantly combine foundational educational theory with a practical collection of resources and case studies on digital teaching, learning, and assessment. Evidence-based strategies guide administrators, faculty, and instructional support staff on how to navigate rapidly evolving educational technologies and enable customized learning for individual students. Comprehensive chapters by experts provide roadmaps for successful development and implementation of teaching, learning and assessment technologies, not just for today, but far into the future."
—**Monica Devanas**, *Director, Teaching Evaluation and Faculty Development Center for Teaching Advancement and Assessment Research, Rutgers University*

Keeping Us Engaged

Student Perspectives (and Research-Based Strategies) on What Works and Why Christine Harrington and 50 College Students

Foreword by José Antonio Bowen

"*Keeping Us Engaged* is beneficial for both novice and seasoned educators. It includes foundational strategies that characterize what it means to an effective educator. The student narratives provide perspectives that reinforce the strategies and clearly translate the practices from theory to impact. The guiding questions at the end of each chapter encourage reflection that hopefully will lead to improved student outcomes.

(Continued from preceding page)

This book should be included in all teacher education programs."—*Tia Brown McNair*, *EdD, Vice President for Diversity, Equity, and Student Success and Executive Director for the TRHT Campus Centers, Association of American Colleges & Universities*

"Student voices matter to shape an educational experience that best supports student learning. Harrington's book is rich in the theory of what makes for an excellent classroom environment. But what distinguishes the book is the detailed stories told by students that illustrate, so compellingly, the value of engagement. Students describe how faculty have created learning environments that help them navigate the messiness of education in ways that are not only supported by what we know about how students learn, but also by the phenomenological experience of so many students from so many different backgrounds. This book is a terrific read for anyone who cares about students and their effective learning in higher education."—*Chris Hakala*, *Director, Center for Excellence in Teaching, Learning, and Scholarship; and Professor of Psychology, Springfield College*

Degrees That Matter

Moving Higher Education to a Learning Systems Paradigm

Natasha A. Jankowski and David W. Marshall

"This book is an important reminder of the necessity for college and university actors to become aware of the critical role they play in the construction of effective learning environments. The authors advocate for a renewed sense of agency where students, faculty, and administrators do not succumb to a culture of compliance. The authors not only ask for a more active and conscious participation in the construction of learning environments, but also for a more honest and public dialogue about the dynamics that work or do not work in higher education institutions. This book is required reading for educational leaders who want to construct creative, caring, and collaborative forms of learning in higher education institutions."—*Teachers College Record*

(Continues on previous page)